The Training of Prison Governors

This book, first published in 1983, examines in detail the training of the key group of people within the British prison system: prison governors. It shows how problems, endemic to the prison system, influences their training; how staff seek to construct a coherent training course and how recruits struggle to come to terms with their ambiguous new role. It describes how attitudes towards the job changed during the training period and argues that the lack of a clear role0image prevented the adoption of a common occupational culture.

The Training of Prison Governors

P.A.J. Waddington

Routledge
Taylor & Francis Group

First published in 1983
by Croom Helm Ltd

This edition first published in 2022 by Routledge
4 Park Square, Milton Park, Abingdon, Oxon, OX14 4RN

and by Routledge
605 Third Avenue, New York, NY 10017

Routledge is an imprint of the Taylor & Francis Group, an informa business

Publisher's Note
The publisher has gone to great lengths to ensure the quality of this reprint but points out that some imperfections in the original copies may be apparent.

Disclaimer
The publisher has made every effort to trace copyright holders and welcomes correspondence from those they have been unable to contact.

A Library of Congress record exists under ISBN: 070992786X

ISBN: 978-1-032-27302-0 (hbk)
ISBN: 978-1-003-29291-3 (ebk)
ISBN: 978-1-032-27461-4 (pbk)

Book DOI 10.4324/9781003292913

THE TRAINING OF PRISON GOVERNORS

ROLE AMBIGUITY AND SOCIALIZATION

P.A.J. WADDINGTON

Published in association with
THE LONDON SCHOOL OF ECONOMICS
AND POLITICAL SCIENCE

CROOM HELM
London & Canberra

©1983 P.A.J. Waddington
Croom Helm Ltd, Provident House, Burrell Row,
Beckenham, Kent BR3 1AT
Croom Helm Australia, PO Box 391, Manuka,
ACT 2603, Australia

British Library Cataloguing in Publication Data

Waddington, P.A.J.
    The training of prison governors.
    1. Prisons——Great Britain——Officials and employees
    I. Title
    365'.023'41   HV9470

    ISBN 0-7099-2786-X

Printed and bound in Great Britain by
Biddles Ltd, Guildford and King's Lynn

CONTENTS

For Diane

TABLES AND FIGURES

Tables

Figures

FOREWORD

This book describes the training of prison assistant
governors as it was during the early 1970s. Compared to others that have been the subject of
research this training course may appear unusually
ineffective. So it was. Whether it was unusual
compared to the generality of other training courses
is, however, a more debateable point. Although I
have no hard evidence to support it, my view is that
the training of assistant governors differed very
little from the training for many other occupations,
especially the newer, so-called, 'semi-professions',
particularly those whose theoretical basis rests on
the social sciences. Many of these occupations
share the obscruity and ambiguity that surrounded
the role of the assistant governor. They also share
the difficulties of establishing the relevance of
social science to the problems likely to be
encountered in practice.
        As the Prison Service have asked me to point
out, the training of assistant governors was
radically revised immediately after the fieldwork
for this research was completed. It is no longer an
eight-month residential course. The period of
residential training at the Staff College, though
remaining the same in aggregate, is now spread over
two years, interspersed by periods of work as
assistant governor in penal establishments. Despite
these changes, I doubt whether the situation has, in
fact, so radically changed. The role of assistant
governor is no less obscure or ambiguous, and the
social sciences are no more relevant, than was the
case when this research was conducted. A series of
short sojourns at the Staff College may be easier
for recruits to bear, without being any more effective.
        Curiously, it is this lack of effectiveness

which is the main significance of assistant governor
training for the social sciences. Sociologists are
often too glib in supposing that socialization is
inevitable. If members of an occupation are found
to share certain social characteristics or to behave
in similar ways, it is tempting to attribute these
similarities to their having been socialized. What
assistant governor training teaches us is that this
is in no way a foregone conclusion. Some occupations do seem to exert a powerful influence upon
their new members, there is ample research testimony
that that is so. However, this does not mean that
all occupations exert a comparable influence upon
those they recruit. Despite good prime facie
reasons for supposing that it would, the Prison
Service did not exert a significant influence upon
its assistant governor recruits. In seeking to
explain why some occupations do, and others do not,
exert an influence upon their members, it is
necessary to move away from the notion that some
'succeed' whilst others 'fail'.

The lack of effectiveness in assistant governor
socialization is also of practical significance.
Ten years after the fieldwork for this research was
completed, those who were then recruits are now
occupying positions of increasing responsibility
within the Prison Service. They share responsibility for a penal system which, by common consent, is
currently facing the most acute crisis in its history. They must cope with the daily consequences of
overcrowding, delapidated buildings, growing numbers
of long-term prisoners, and the vicissitudes of
unimaginative penal policy. In a less optimistic
intellectual climate, the belief in rehabilitation
that sustained the previous generation of governor
grades, is no longer credible. Prisons are now
recognized, to quote the former governor of Wormwood
Scrubs, as 'social dustbins'. Yet, it is precisely
because conditions are so appalling and apparently
hopeless that it is important that men and women who
are committed to maintaining civilized and humane
standards continue to be recruited into positions of
responsibility within the Prison Service.

I completed my four-year association with the
Prison Service holding those who staffed it, at all
levels, in very high regard. They fulfilled their
unenviable roles with greater humanity, robust good
sense and humour than any of us outside the Service
had any reason to expect. If the Prison Service
failed to force its governor grades into a common
mould, this is not, in my view, a ground for critic-

ism, but reason for hope.

P.A.J.W.

ACKNOWLEDGEMENTS

Inevitably, during the course of this research I have become indebted to more people than I can possibly mention. To them all I give my thanks. There are, however, a few to whom I am particularly indebted.

First, I am indebted to the Prison Service, especially the Central Training Organization, and most especially of all the staff of the Staff College. Without the help of Colonel 'Jim' Haywood and Mr. R.S. Llewellyn and the continued cooperation of Mr. W.J. Booth, this research would have been impossible. Without the assistance of the librarians, secretarial and clerical staff of the College, it would have been far more arduous.

Of course, I owe a particular debt of gratitude to the tutors, lecturers, and staff at various penal establishments as well as Social Service and Probation Departments, who allowed me to observe assistant governor training at first hand.

Most of all, I am indebted to those recruits who willingly completed questionnaires, allowed me to interview them and cheerfully accepted me as one of them during the period of my observations.

Second, there are those without whose continued help and guidance I would have been unable to make sense of the mountain of data I collected. My former Head of Department and Professor, Norman Jepson, not only used his deserved reputation within the Prison Service to obtain their cooperation and funding, but despite the many competing demands on his time, continued to take a close interest in the research throughout. The late Mr. Arthur Royce helped to steer me through the complexities of statistical analysis. Dr. Tom Nossiter refused to allow any unsubstantiated or ill-considered notion to go unchallenged and maintained my interest in

this topic even when it felt like an uphill struggle.
Without his help I am sure that this research would
never have seen the light of day. Latterly, Mr.
Peter Schofield has critically read the earlier
drafts of this book in an effort to render them into
plain English. To each of these friends and
colleagues I give my special thanks.

Of course, it goes without saying that despite
the invaluable help I have received from these and
others, I accept sole responsibility for what is
written here.

Chapter One

SOCIALIZATION THEORY AND PRISON GOVERNORS

INTRODUCTION

Prison governors and assistant governors do not
readily spring to mind as objects of social psychological or sociological research. Beyond the relatively narrow confines of the British Prison
Services, few will have been more than aware of
their existence, since what these governor grades of
the Prison Service actually do and the kind of
people they are, are normally concealed behind
prison walls. Despite this obscurity they are not
unimportant, for prison governor grades form the
most senior tier of staff within the Prison Services,
responsible for the day-to-day functioning of penal
establishments with a total of over 40,000 inmates.
However, it is not primarily to their penological
significance that this research is addressed, but
the sociological and social psychological implications of their initial training.
     Occupational socialization refers to the
process through which people acquire such social
characteristics as distinctive attitudes, when they
enter an occupation. Assistant governors, the rank
at which virtually all governor grades are inducted,
are important in this context because they differ
quite markedly from those occupations which have
preoccupied socialization research - such as medicine, nursing, the military and law - in that they
lack a clear public image. The question that will
be asked throughout this book will be: is the model
of socialization traditionally used by sociologists
generalizable to an occupation whose image is not
clearly or consensually defined even to those who
are most directly involved, the recruits and the
training staff? If it is not, then we may need to

consider some reformulation of orthodox socialization theory.

Such a question is important not only to academic social science, but also to those who organize
the growing number of occupational training courses
in the 'human relations' field, such as social work
and personnel management. Like assistant governors,
such occupations may have yet to establish an agreed
conception of their role amongst the occupation's
membership. Also, like assistant governors, such
occupations may be dependent upon the social
sciences for their theoretical background and may
share the difficulties in establishing the relevance
of the training course for later practice. Does
orthodox socialization theory, with its emphasis on
the power of initial training to mould recruits'
social orientations, provide sound guidance for the
organization of such courses, or is a more complex
model necessary?

These are the broad issues to which this book
is addressed. It examines the social psychological
consequences of the initial training of assistant
governors, and seeks some understanding of the
social processes responsible for them. The particular occupation need not have been assistant governors in order to have explored these broader
implications, but the circumstances surrounding the
training of assistant governors provides a clear
opportunity to do so.

In this introductory chapter it is necessary,
therefore, to describe the prevailing model of
socialization and to explain why assistant governors
provide a good prime facie opportunity to assess its
adequacy. How the research was designed to test the
theory will also be explained.

THE THEORY OF OCCUPATIONAL SOCIALIZATION

The question of why members of a society overwhelm-
ingly conform to the norms and values of their
culture despite the absence or patent ineffective-
ness of overt controls, has long been a central
issue in sociological theory.[1] The prevailing orthodoxy attempts to solve this conundrum by maintaining that social systems ensure individual compliance
through a person's internalization of norms and
values. This process of socialization leads men to
adopt cultural patterns as their own personal
standards of proper conduct.[2] Whilst the major
emphasis of theory and research has been upon the

socialization of children, the theory applies with no less force to the induction of new members into any group or organization, including occupations.[3] In complex industrial societies where adult social positions cannot be predicted with certainty for a child and, therefore, appropriate socialization cannot be provided as it can in a social system based upon ascription, secondary socialization becomes all the more significant.[4]

Although socialization into occupations is less far reaching than childhood socialization, usually requiring the inculcation of relatively specific norms and values, it is thought to follow the same general process, namely the transformation of a relatively heterogeneous collection of individuals into a functionally homogeneous group. This is the view adopted by Merton in his classic definition of socialization as 'the process by which people selectively acquire the values and attitudes, the interests, skills and knowledge - in short, the culture - current in the group of which they are, or seek to become, a member. It refers to the learning of social roles'.[5] Such a definition assumes that groups are homogeneous and distinctive and that, therefore, as individuals change their membership of groups, they also change their social characteristics.

Certainly such a view is not without empirical support, even if the assumption of the malleability of human behaviour may seem to some to be contrary to commonsense. Lieberman found,[6] for example, that those workers who were promoted to foremen or elected as shop stewards became, respectively, more or less pro-management in their attitudes compared to their former colleagues who remained as workers. Moreover, following a recession in the industry which led to some of the foremen returning to the ranks of the ordinary workers, and also following elections which resulted in some shop stewards reverting to their former status, he found that the attitudes of these men changed again, so as to become similar once more, to those of ordinary workers. Such evidence has been taken as supporting the view that people's attitudes and behaviour can be more or less moulded at will to conform to the norms and values of the groups of which they are, or are about to become, a member.

It is important to recognize that this is not merely an incidental fact of social life, but is, in the view of socialization theorists, an essential social process. It is socialization that is mainly responsible for the continuing integration of the social system by ensuring that the system itself does not change as its membership changes. As Kingsley Davis puts it, 'The paradox of human society - that it has a unity and a continuity of its own and yet exists solely in the minds and actions of its members - can be resolved only by understanding how the new born individual is moulded into a social being'.[7] In other words, social systems remain integrated and stable by moulding their ever changing membership to meet their requirements, that is transforming them into 'good working members'.[8] Clausen describes this outcome thus: 'From the perspective of the larger society, the individual can be said to be socialized when he has learned to think and feel in the ways that someone of his age, sex and placement is supposed to think and feel ...'.[9]

In an occupational context we would, therefore, expect that recruits would necessarily acquire the various social characteristics required for the maintenance of the occupational culture, in both its formal and informal aspects. This will be achieved, it is argued, by complex, yet imperceptible, processes embedded in the minutiae of the recruit's initial experience of the role.

An example of this approach is provided by Renee Fox's 1957 study of the socialization of Columbia medical students.[10] It is claimed to be a functional requirement of medicine that doctors be tolerant of the pervasive uncertainty that characterizes practise, but this tolerance has to be learned, since students tend to have an inflated expectation of the power of medical science. They learn it, claims Fox, through various subtle processes of socialization, such as the refusal of their teachers to 'spoon-feed' them medical knowledge, requiring, instead, that they discover things for themselves which, incidentally, leads them to discover the complexity and lack of standardization in the human organism. Later in their training they may follow the case of a terminally ill patient, and as they await the eventual death and subsequent post-mortem, they will learn that prognosis is insufficiently precise even to predict the time of death and, when they attend the autopsy, they find that diagnosis is so uncertain that it is often in error and invariably incomplete. Through these and other similar experiences the student comes to accept the limitations under which he must work.

Orthodox theorists would argue that Fox's study

illustrates the most important features of the
socialization process as it is experienced by those
undergoing it, that is, its latency and its diffuseness. Latency refers to the implicit, unintended,
incidental nature of much socialization. Medical
students are not instructed to be tolerant of
uncertainty, but acquire tolerance as an unintended
by-product of other, planned and unplanned aspects
of their training. In part, it is the latency of
much socialization that is responsible, or so it is
argued, for the extraordinary influence that it has
upon social behaviour, for in being conveyed in this
insidious manner, artefacts of social life are
treated as the unavoidable natural facts of human
existence. We do not learn, or so we believe, that
incest is wrong, its abhorrence to us is natural and
inevitable, but according to socialization theory,[11]
even such deeply ingrained taboos as this are indeed
socially acquired.

The diffuseness of socialization is usually
less important in the context of occupational
socialization, for it refers to the ways in which
social characteristics acquired in one role can
influence behaviour elsewhere. The most extensively
researched examples of this have been orthodox
studies of political socialization,[12] for although
there is very little socialization into the citi-
zen's role as such, people appear to acquire appropriate political orientations in the course of their
participation in other social roles such as in the
family, at school and at work. For occupational
socialization, 'diffuseness' is usually restricted
to the fact that characteristics acquired in a
training school, for example, should continue to
influence behaviour when the person has ceased to be
a student and is a fully-fledged member of the
occupation itself.

This brings us to the other side of the socialization process – the agents who mediate the social
system's influence by transmitting the culture to
the neophyte. The agent may be no more aware that
he is transmitting cultural expectations than the
neophyte is that he is learning them. Indeed,
according to Clausen, socialization is an implicit
part of all social interaction: '... every enduring
relationship may be said to entail socialization,
for every enduring relationship entails a building
up of mutual expectations which become to a degree
normative for the participants'.[13] Moreover, agents
have a vested interest in ensuring effective self-
control in those they socialize, since this will

reduce the need for continuous surveillance and control of those who cannot or will not control themselves,[14] resulting in socialization.

The orthodox theory claims that in adult life, the socializing agents who come closest to the paradigm case of parents, both in the degree of surveillance and the ability to control the behaviour of those they are socializing, are the staff of what have been called 'assimilating institutions'[15] - residential training organizations which are able to cut off recruits from possible outside influences and expose them to intensive socialization from the staff of the organization.[16] Unlike other socializing agents who are responsible for the socialization of adults, those in such organizations have little to fear from incompatible influences impinging upon the individual. As Dornbusch, who coined the term 'assimilating institution', observed of the coastguard academy,[17] even other recruits could be counted on to enforce the expectations of the organization.

Thus, it would appear from this perspective that entering an occupation necessarily involves socialization, especially where that is accompanied by a period in a residential training organization, during which those entering the occupation from more or less diverse backgrounds acquire the social characteristics of their new group. Such a theory is merely the specific application of general socialization theory which assumes that those being socialized are passive recipients of their culture, capable of infinite malleability as they pass from group to group. The process is, therefore, assumed to be one of unidirectional influence by agents upon those to whom they transmit the culture, with the result that the latter will share as completely as is possible the values and norms of the group, essential to the continued functioning of that group as a social system.

This is the theory, but it is certainly not one that is universally accepted. Dennis Wrong's influential critique has long branded such a view as an 'over-socialized conception of man',[18] dehumanizing in its implications. Yet, despite this and other criticisms, which draw attention to its implicit reification and teleology,[19] the theory continues to be the prevailing orthodoxy, as any review of contemporary research will confirm.[20] Some researchers, it is true, acknowledge the problem of 'over-socialization', but nevertheless continue to maintain that the orthodox model is, at least, partially applicable, even if it does not explain the whole process of socialization[21]   Others have abandoned these orthodox assumptions entirely, adopting an alternative model of socialization for the purposes of empirical research,[22] emphasizing a more active role for the recipients of socialization, but valuable though such studies have been, they have failed to invalidate the orthodox theory, since they have not shown that it is incapable of explaining the empirical facts that they have observed. Indeed, there are very few empirical tests of orthodox socialization theory at all, conducted either by proponents or critics. Amongst proponents of the theory, the model is largely assumed to be correct and either applied to describe a process of socialization or to explain retrospectively how members of a group must have acquired the characteristics they possess.[23] On the other hand, there is no denying that some groups do seem capable of ensuring that their members share common social characteristics. The empirical issue is whether this is inevitably true of all occupational groups, or whether there are some that fail to conform to the model and, if so, why? This is an issue that can only be resolved by an empirical test of the theory.

An occupation which merits attention in this regard is that of assistant governor (AG) in the British Prison Service, for the circumstances of their occupational socialization amounts to a stringent test of the theory.

ASSISTANT GOVERNORS

The English Prison Service,[24] or, to be more precise, the Prison Department of the Home Office, as it was at the time of this research, administers all the prisons, borstals and detention centres in England and Wales. As such it was, at the time of this research, responsible for the custody, treatment and training of around 40,000 inmates in 135 establishments.[25]

The Prison Service was administered by the Home Office and was divided into male and female establishments, and borstals and prisons. Prisons and borstals were somewhat separately organized, for example, there were separate statutory rules for each, although this did not prevent or inhibit transfers of staff. There were a variety of types of establishment performing different functions, such as that between open and closed borstals which

reflected their relative security. Within prisons,
local prisons and remand centres performed the
function of servicing the courts by holding prisoners on remand and receiving them after sentence,
imprisoning short-term prisoners and allocating long
-term prisoners. Training prisons were those that
received long-term prisoners and these were, in turn,
distinguished according to the security classific-
ation of the prisoners they held, from 'Category A',
who were maximum security prisoners such as murder-
ers and terrorists, to 'Category D' who were suitable for open conditions.

Prison Service staff formed a two-tier hierarchy, comparable to the military distinction
between 'officers' and 'other ranks'. Confusingly,
the 'officers' in the Prison Service form the lower
tier comprising the vast majority of staff, known
throughout the Service as 'discipline grades'. In
prisons they are uniformed, but at that time those
in borstals were not. They are divided into the
ranks of Chief Officers (classes I and II), Principal Officers, Senior Officers, and Basic Grade
Officers. The senior grades are divided into five
ranks, designated at that time, Governors classes I,
II and III, and Assistant Governors classes I and II.
Above them are Controllers and Regional Directors,
and beneath them the discipline grades. In the
largest prisons the normal complement would be a
Governor I acting as governor, a Governor III as
deputy, possibly an AGI acting as second deputy, and
one AGII to each wing.[26] In smaller establishments
the same pattern would be more or less retained with
a reduction in the seniority of staff at each level,
so that the typical complement of an average borstal
would have been a Governor III governor, an AGI
deputy, and one AGII per house acting as housemaster.

Obscurity and Diversity

At the time of this research, AGs spent the first
eight months of their career at the Prison Service
Staff College, Wakefield, on a residential training
course which had the declared aim of providing them
with a combination of theoretical knowledge and
practical skills necessary to perform their duties.
If socialization theory is indeed adequate, there is
every reason to suppose that AGs would be socialized
during this period of induction into their new role.

In combining theoretical and practical training,
the course at the Staff College had the central
characteristics of socialization in the professions,

which is noted for its effectiveness in inculcating an occupational culture. In wider respects, the socialization of AGs has some features similar to those of the military officer caste. AGs are a small elite within a uniformed, disciplined, para-military organization, responsible for the socially important, often difficult and sometimes dangerous task of containing prisoners whom they are also supposed to rehabilitate. Like both professionals and the military, the AG's occupation is, in Stanton Wheeler's terms,[27] not only a role, it is also a status, which means that its members are not simply required to perform certain duties, but be a type of person. Therefore, socialization must have quite a profound influence upon recruits and give them the attitudes and values that will transform them into the required type. Finally, the intense, residential course at the Staff College has some of the features of an 'assimilating institution',[28] and although it may lack the systematic intimidation and brutality known as 'hazing', its segregation of recruits from normal life outside the College and their immersion in the occupational milieu, might be expected to have a significant effect upon recruits.

On the other hand, there were important features of the AG's occupation and training which suggested that this was not so, and makes their socialization a severe test of the theory. First, the AG is a distinctly obscure occupation, in the sense that few are aware of its existence, especially when compared to nursing, medicine, the military and other occupations upon which socialization theorists have mainly concentrated their research. Some occupations become socially visible through the mass media portrayal of them in either drama or documentary, but until recently there have been few popular television programmes which portrayed prison work at all, and even those that did have tended to ignore governor grades, especially AGs. Other occupations become socially visible through the direct relationship that many members of the society have with them. Thus, although the mass media also pays relatively little attention to schools and teaching, virtually everyone will know something of the teacher's role from their own experience as pupils.

From these sources of information people form an image of the occupation and it does not matter whether this image is accurate, provided it is common to all prospective recruits and gives them a coherent orientation. For example, Ida Simpson has pointed out[29] that student nurses enter that occup-

ation with an inaccurate, idealistic view of the
role as involving only the bedside care of patients.
Throughout their socialization they must divest
themselves of such an image and come to value technical competence and administrative aspects of the
role which tend to distance them from a personal
relationship with the patient. On the other hand,
Mary Jo Huntingdon has argued[30] that medical students constructively use their stereotyped image of
the doctor to rehearse their professional self-image
by presenting themselves as 'doctors' to patients
and other laymen. This they can do by wearing the
stereotyped white coat, with the stethoscope poking
conspicuously out of the pocket. Whether inaccurate
or not, whether a hindrance or a help, the public
image of the occupation gave both sets of students
some common point of reference for the future.
Where, however, there is no agreed public image of
the occupation, recruits may enter without any
common impression of what they are to become and
socializing agents too may find it difficult to
influence recruits when they have no clear notion of
what recruits believe about the occupation, whether
inaccurate or not.

A second feature of the AG's occupation which
may prevent effective socialization is its diversity,
that is, AGs perform a wide variety of duties in
various establishments. In the traditional borstal,
for example, an AG housemaster would be responsible
for a 'house' and its 60 to 80 resident trainees.
The house is the basic unit of such a borstal and
the housemaster's duties and responsibilities are
set out in the Borstal Rules. Yet there have been
borstal regimes in which the AG had no responsibilities for a house as such, but only for a 'caseload'
of trainees, with whom he was supposed to have a
specialized social casework relationship. In
prisons, an AG does not exist at all according to
the Prison Rules, his role being entirely dependent
upon the delegated authority of the governor. Different governors have employed prison AGs in various
ways in different establishments. In a long-term
training prisons, AGs may well be responsible for a
wing and the inmates resident there, but the wing of
a prison does not usually enjoy the same importance
as does the house in a borstal, and so the AG is
just one amongst a variety of specialists, including
security officers, prison welfare officers, industrial managers. In a local prison, or remand centre,
the AG's duties will be largely administrative and
although he may have notional responsibility for a

wing, he would have little opportunity to develop
relationships amongst a rapidly changing inmate
population. AGs are also employed in the interviewing and allocation of borstal trainees at one of the
two Borstal Allocation Centres.

Later in their careers, AGs could be employed
at Head Office or one of the regional offices in a
purely administrative capacity. Equally, they could
be training either discipline officers or AG
recruits at one of the three training establishments.

In other words, there is little that is uniform
to the role of the AG, but this, perhaps, would not
be so significant were there also not considerable
controversy about the type of person the AG ought to
be. This controversy stems from the origins of the
AG's role and is deeply enmeshed within the wider
arguments that surround the Prison Service.

The Historical Context - Ambiguity and Controversy
The forerunner of the AG, the borstal tutor, was
introduced into the Prison Service in 1909 as part
of the whole borstal ethos which attempted to get
away from the militarism of the adult prison system.[31]
It was symbolic of changing penal philosophy,
following the Gladstone Committee's report of 1895,
in which rehabilitation was to be the primary goal
of the prison system and governors were to be the
major rehabilitators through their personal contact
with inmates.

As the borstal system expanded and developed it
became increasingly modelled upon the English Public
School, with all staff abandoning uniform and some
borstals eventually becoming 'open' establishments,
that is, with a markedly lower degree of security.
The regime of these borstals, especially between the
two World Wars, was unapologetically paternalistic,
recently described as 'muscular Christianity, with
bags of dedication and healthy exercise in the fresh
air'.[32] Its central agent was the tutor, restyled
as the housemaster during the 1920s, who was offic-
ially recognised by the Borstal Rules as performing
a distinct function in the rehabilitation of the
inmates in his house. As the Advisory Council on
the Treatment of Offenders later described the AG:

> He is, under the Governor, responsible not only
> for the general administration of his House,
> but also for the personal training and guidance
> of each of fifty or more boys comprising it.
> Thus, the basic responsibility for the success
> of borstal training rests upon his shoulders;

he must be aware of the outside influences that
may have some bearing on the boy's delinquency
or affect his attitude to society, and with
which the boy may have to contend when he goes
out.[33]

He was also described by a serving housemaster as
'everything and nothing',[34] but it was precisely the
all-embracing and diffuse quality of the role that
ensured that it was central to the borstal system.

So long as the borstal system flourished and
continued to expand, the housemaster's role also was
enhanced. Given that he was the central agent of
this successful arm of the prison system, it made
sense to introduce the role into other parts of that
system where, perhaps, he could disseminate the
rehabilitative ethic. Gradually, the role of housemaster, but now renamed as AG, began to appear in
training prisons and increasingly after World War
Two in virtually every type of establishment within
the system.

Not only was the AG's role dispersed throughout
the system, the status of the role within the Prison
Service changed. In 1934, Sir Lionel Fox's account
of the Service[35] makes no mention of the housemaster
in connection with the 'superior officers' of the
Service, but by 1952 he announces[36] with some pride
that the rank of AG has become fully-established as
the near-exclusive avenue for promotion to governor.

If the dissemination of the role throughout the
Service and its increased status was a measure of
the AG's growing importance, it also created the
difficulties that were to afflict the role thereafter. Firstly, dissemination implied that the
housemaster had some distinctive contribution to
make to the rest of the prison system, whereas, in
fact, the role was inextricably linked to the ethos
and organization of the borstal system. Removed
from that milieu the housemaster lost the distinct-
iveness of the role, since even in a training prison
the wing is not the central unit that the borstal
house is, and, therefore, to be placed in charge of
such a wing is not to perform a central function
within the establishment.

Moreover, unlike the housemaster in a borstal,
the AG in a prison is not recognised by the Prison
Rules which has contributed to the ambiguity of the
position. Before AGs were introduced into prisons,
the staff structure at least had the merit of being
uncomplicated, with the chain of command running
from the Governor through his deputy and the Chief
Officer to the basic grade staff. But now, where was

the AG to fit in? For example, did his responsibility for a prison wing entail control over the uniformed staff working there? This responsibility had traditionally and formally been that of the Chief Officer, who retained it, but then in what sense was the AG 'in charge' of the wing? Furthermore, since the avenue of promotion from Chief Officer class I was the same as that for an AGII, that is, to AGI, were they to be considered of collateral status within the staff hierarchy when the AGII was a governor grade and the Chief Officer a discipline grade?

In addition to these organizational difficulties, there was, secondly, the confusion about whether the AG was a role or a rank. The position had been disseminated throughout the prison system apparently in order to spread the rehabilitative ethic, which implied that it was a distinctive role, but at the same time, it had become the main promotion channel for all governors, which implied that it was a rank. The difference is more than semantic, for if it was a role it could be expected to have a distinctive organizational contribution, but if it was a rank, then AGs might undertake any of the responsibilities delegated to them by their superior ranks, in part as a means of training them for later promotion. (This at least is the view of the Governors' association[37]). However, this conflict has not been resolved, despite attempts to do so, and the occupation of the AG retains both the elements of a role and a rank.

More insidious still has been the growing suspicion amongst many concerned with penal affairs during recent years about the value of the rehabilitative ethic itself. One consequence of this has been to undermine the role historically so closely associated with it. The Prison Service has steadily given less weight to rehabilitation as an aim of penal policy,[38] partly as a result of increasing reconviction rates amongst former inmates of borstals,[39] but also influenced by changes in academic criminological thinking.[40] Furthermore, those employed within the system have expressed themselves more sceptical of its merits.[41] This further contributed to the ambiguity of the role, since as AGs were supposedly spreading the commitment to rehabilitation throughout the Service, that commitment was itself declining.

Thus, it seems, the role of AG has been a victim of its own success, expanding only to find that this expansion led the role into ambiguity and

confusion. This is apparent not only to the outside
observer, but also to those within the governor
grades themselves. It would indeed be fair to say
that they have, during recent years, agonised, sometimes publicly, about the problems of the AG's role.
The governors' official staff association described
it as a 'troubled' role in its evidence to a House
of Commons Select Committee;[42] a former Controller
of Operations (one of the most senior positions in
the Prison Service), complained that AGs have 'been
left over the years with residual odds and ends' and
was joined in his complaints by a, then, Regional
Director who observed that 'One of the conflicts
about the role of Assistant Governor is the lack of
decision as to whether he should be responsible for
a place and a group of people, or a function';[43] and
the debate about the role has been pursued in the
columns of the Prison Service Journal,[44] not to
mention many unpublished internal memoranda.[45]

Attempted Solutions for Role Ambiguity

Historically, there have been two principal
solutions advanced for these difficulties: either
redefining the AG as a specialist rehabilitator, or
as a general manager, both of which exploit different attributes of the traditional housemaster's role.

The first solution to be advanced (during the
early 1960s) was that of the AG as an institutional
social caseworker, rehabilitating inmates through
the use of interpersonal skills modelled along the
lines of social workers. This view involves a
continuing commitment to the rehabilitative ethic
and primacy of the AG as a rehabilitative agent, but
seeks to give the AG a specific rather than diffuse
role within the establishment. It was fully accepted when the Advisory Council on the Treatment of
Offenders in 1966 recommended[46] that this should be
the major component of the AG's role, to be followed
shortly afterwards by the announcement of the Prison
Department to the Commons Select Committee[47] of a
training course designed to equip new AGs to perform
this task.

There were a number of problems associated with
this plan which may or may not have caused its
abandonment. First, the inherent difficulty of
separating a rehabilitative function from all the
other functions within an establishment meant that
this solution would not give to AGs the desired
measure of role-specificity. A prison or borstal is
an institution in which prisoners spend their entire

life whilst imprisoned and rehabilitation will, presumably, result from the inmate's total experience within it, and therefore if the AG were to be responsible for rehabilitation he would need to have control of the inmate's total experience, a measure of authority unlikely to be granted to a junior grade of staff. Second, there were the practical difficulties arising from the conflict that ensued between these aspirations of AGs and those of the newly-introduced prison welfare officers. This conflict arose[48] because AGs were perceived to be encroaching into the social casework field for which PWOs were formally qualified and AGs were not. Since PWOs were seconded probation officers only temporarily assigned to a prison whilst retaining their accountability to their superiors in the Probation Service, they were able to buttress their case by appealing to their professional peers outside of the Service for support. The idea of training AGs as social caseworkers was eventually dropped and was followed in the mid-1970s by a proposal to introduce PWOs into borstals also,[49] thereby strengthening their claim to be the specialists exclusively concerned with social casework.

The Prison Department did not implement the plans they had announced to the Select Committee and the emphasis shifted from redefining the AG's role as social casework to that of seeing him as a manager. This emphasis harked back to the diffuse responsibility the housemaster had had for the total institutional experience of his 'lads' and incorporated the notion of the AG as a rank rather than a role. Ideally, AGs should share the general responsibilities of the governor for the establishment as a whole, but here, too, there were entrenched interests. First, the aspiration to have managerial control implied control over the main resource of any penal establishment, its staff, but this had been and remained the responsibility of the Chief Officer who arranged the 'detail' - where officers were to work and their duties - and who was also responsible for writing Officers' annual reports, and was more experienced in the Service. Whilst attempts have been made to reorganize the relationship between these two roles, these have as yet been unsuccessful.[50]

Second, and according to the same logic, AGs should have a share in the administration of the establishment, for which the governor has overall responsibility, but which is actually undertaken by the Administration Officer (A.O.), a seconded civil

servant. Again, AGs' claims in this direction have
met with considerable resistance from AOs,[51] who
have managed to retain their special area of
responsibility.

Because of these difficulties, very little
actually changed in the AG's role, despite this the
Prison Service insisted that their role was indeed
to be defined as that of a manager. This trend can
readily be discerned by the changing emphasis in the
recruitment advertisements, which in 1967 read,
'Duties demand a lively interest in social problems,
and a good understanding of modern methods of
handling them'. To be replaced in 1969 by: 'Are you
interested in social work? Could you also - with
the right training - do a good managerial job?'.
Which was changed in 1972 to:

> Management with a Social Purpose
> As an Assistant Governor you are primarily a
> manager. You will organize, train and support
> the staff through whom you are responsible for
> the entire existence of a group of offenders in
> custody. As you may have to deal personally
> with the problems of your charges, you must be
> able to recognise their needs and have know-
> ledge of the specialist skills and resources
> available for their treatment and rehabilit-
> ation.

Thus, the role for which recruits were being
socialized was itself confused and surrounded by
controversy, but the implications of this wider
situation had a more direct bearing upon the training of recruits than this alone, for the question of
what training to give AG recruits became increasingly entwined in the controversy about the role.

The Development of Training
Originally, the training of AGs was restricted to
ex-officers only (those promoted from the discipline
grades), and is remembered in Prison Service folklore as being designed to transform 'other ranks'
into 'gentlemen', an interpretation given substance
by the course reports of the period.[52] The courses
given were expressly not designed to provide
professional training. Sir Lionel Fox made this
plain as recently as 1952, when he said that their
'purpose however is not so much to give professional
training as to test the capacity of minds and
personality to develop and respond to such training'[53]. What this actually meant was that the
courses concentrated upon instruction in the liberal

arts, such as history, literature and musical appre-
cation. If those on the courses satisfied their
tutors, they were then confirmed as AGs, but not all
of them did so and the unsuccessful had to return to
the discipline grades or leave the Service.

For direct-entrants, who could, presumably,
already be counted upon to be gentlemen, there was
no such course. Such training as there was took
place in their first posting augmented by what was
known throughout the Service as 'the Grand Tour',
during which the recruit would visit a number of
establishments with a view to familiarizing himself
with the system, and a short course at the Staff
College, Wakefield, to mark the end of the probationary period.

Antiquated though this may now appear, it was a
system attuned to its time, reflecting the fact that
governor grades in the inter-war and immediate post-
war period were not considered as specialists in
particular functional areas, but a kind of person
who could be entrusted with the diffuse responsibilities of the role.

The watershed came in 1958 when the segregation
of direct-entrants and ex-officers was brought to an
end by the inclusion of the former on the Staff
Course. This change, however, necessitated a reapp-
raisal of the content of the course, since clearly
it would no longer be appropriate to provide a
smattering of culture to the already cultured. The
result was that the course included ever increasing
amounts of social science to the eventual exclusion
of the liberal arts, the justification for which was
that this was professionally relevant knowledge[54].
This was formally recognised in 1964 when the
department in the Staff College with responsibility
for the initial training of AGs was given the title
'Social Studies Department'.

At the time that the fieldwork for this research took place there was no disputing the
pretensions of the AG's Course (as the former Staff
Course was now called) to professional status. As
the newspaper advertisement for the AG's job
claimed:

> Training, both academic and practical, will be
> given on joining the Service. A residential
> course at the Staff College, Wakefield, will
> give theoretical training in the form of
> lectures, seminars, tutorials and project work,
> while practical experience will be gained by
> periods of attachment to prisons and borstals
> or young offender institutions. Among the

> subjects covered will be the understanding of
> human behaviour, theory and practice of social
> casework, groupwork, institutional organization
> and management, and instruction in the tech-
> nical aspects of the job.

The social science content was provided by university lecturers who visited the Staff College and
taught courses in sociology, psychology, criminology
and penology, human growth and development, and
management studies.[55]

Whatever the causal connection between them, it
is obvious that the change in emphasis from the
liberal arts to a professional training based upon
the social sciences corresponded well to the claims
by AGs and on their behalf for a functionally
specific role within the Service. Initially, this
was seen to lie in the direction of social casework
training and internal memoranda conveyed the attitude of that time: '... the present trend of the
Staff Course is towards application, with emphasis
on casework training ... We are making gradual
progress towards the goal of making all Assistant
Governors professionally trained'.[56] However, these
hopes were to be dashed by the abandonment of that
development in favour of a management-style alternative, the immediate result of which was that the
AG's Course remained a stop-gap measure until the
mid-1970s,[57] when it was replaced by a 'management-
styled' course.

There were other, more pervasive difficulties
in establishing the professional credentials of such
a course, similar to those that had afflicted other
occupations seeking professional status. This is
not the place to consider the professionalization
process in any detail, except to note that the
sociology of the professions has increasingly turned
away from the 'traits approach' which sought to
describe the objective requirements for professional
status to be conferred on occupations, and paid more
attention to how occupational groups seek to enhance
and protect their position by aspiring to professional status.[58] What this strategy usually involves
is emulating the pattern established by medicine and
law, principally the reliance of these professions
upon the application of an esoteric body of knowledge.[59] Like others, those responsible for training AGs turned to the social sciences as the most
available, and apparently appropriate, source of
such esoteric knowledge, and also like others found
that this created almost as many problems as it
solved.

18

The main difficulty that they encountered was that the social sciences were and, indeed, still are, in no position to provide the definitive basis of knowledge that can act as a prescription for practice. Like other aspirant professions, AGs found themselves in the position described by Wilensky thus:

> All occupations in the human relations field have only tenuous claims to exclusive competence. This results not only from their newness, uncertain standards, and the embryonic state of the social and psychological sciences on which they draw, but also from the fact that the types of problem dealt with are part of everyday living. The lay public cannot recognise the need for special competence in an area where everyone is 'expert'.[60]

These problems become all the more acute when it is not the lay public that an occupation needs to convince of its expertise, but other occupations with whom members of the aspiring profession work.[61]

The dilemma for AGs as much as for other such occupations is that although the social sciences have not produced a definitive basis of knowledge, the acquisition of such knowledge and, at least, the appearance of training, are the prerequisites for the achievement of professional status and acceptance of special competence, and there is no available alternative. Just as other occupations have become disenchanted with their supposedly professional training, so too have AGs. The remarks of the Central Council for Education and Training in Social Work on proposals to teach sociology to social workers, apply no less to AGs than to social workers: 'It is important to stress that students are being "trained". They are more likely to identify with the course if they can see that the knowledge they are gaining can be applied'.[62] If, as is likely, they do not see their training as applicable, then they are unlikely to identify with academic social science and will, therefore, become dissatisfied.

In sum, although the training of AGs appeared to be unproblematic, closer inspection reveals a situation of confusion at all levels. It is unclear what the role was for which they were being trained and the claim of the Staff College to be able to provide quasi-professional training seems highly questionable.

THE RECRUITMENT, SELECTION AND TRAINING OF AGS

It was into this confused situation that AGs were
recruited and trained, and their recruitment and
selection reflected these underlying difficulties.
AGs were recruited from within the discipline grades
of the Service or as direct-entrants, through a
three-day extended interview procedure jointly
organized with the Civil Service Selection Board
(CSSB). Once selected, they attended the Staff
College, Wakefield, for an eight-month course of
theoretical and practical instruction. All recruits
were now treated more or less equally, there being
no further system of selection for ex-officers at
the Staff College as there had been in the past. At
the end of the training course, recruits were
assigned to establishments to work as AGIIs, with a
more or less notional period of probation extending
to the end of the second year of service.
    However, the obscurity and diversity of the
role, and the ambiguity and controversy that surrounded it, as well as the questionable quas-
professional status of the training course, had a
two-fold significance for the effectiveness of the
socialization process. First, these circumstances
have contributed to the relative indeterminacy of
the recruitment process because the occupation is
obscure to the general public, from whom the Service
wished to recruit direct-entrants.[63] Certainly, no
direct-entrant claimed even to have known about the
existence of the job before having their attention
drawn to it either by the advertisement published in
the 'serious' daily newspapers, or an employment
agency, whereupon they decided almost immediately to
apply for the post. This is unlike the pattern
found elsewhere and thought to be typical of occupational choice, which is that prospective applicants spend considerable time prior to making their
job application contemplating which career to enter
and adjusting themselves to this prospect. Amongst
all recruits there was little to suggest that they
had been selectively attracted to the occupation
because it appealed to some common value, or other
social characteristic, which they had in common.[64]
    Even amongst ex-officers, for whom the AG's
role was not so obscure, there were impediments to
the structured self-selection of applicants which
normally ensures that only those with particular
social characteristics apply for an occupation. Ex-
officers had previously worked in a diverse collection of establishments: some had worked in large

local prisons, others in training prisons, yet
others in borstals or detention centres. Given the
diversity of the AG's role, the direct prior knowledge that any individual officer would have of it,
would depend upon the type of establishment in which
he worked. Therefore, since ex-officers were
recruited from different types of establishment,
they could be expected to have different views.
Even this understates the problem, since in some
types of establishment the officer would have a
better opportunity to observe the AG's role, than
would his contemporaries in other types of establishment. Thus, for the officer working in a large
local prison, the AG may be a distant figure about
whom he knows little, or, as one ex-officer
expressed it: 'I saw the AGs going home at 5.30,
knowing that I was going to be there /the prison/
until 9.30'. Indeed, it was this perception of the
working conditions of AGs that ex-officers claimed
was the most important motivation in seeking promotion. It was the improved status, salary, and
conditions of service, together with the belief that
there would be more intrinsic job satisfaction as an
AG, that attracted them, rather than any desire to
perform the specific duties of the AG, about which
they admittedly knew little. What made them believe
that they would be suited to such a job, was not the
correspondence between the requirements of the role
and their own abilities and aptitudes, but the fact
that many had known of other officers who had been
promoted and reasoned that if these others had been
successful, so might they.[65]
     Thus, if the social composition of AG recruits
was to have a distinctive pattern, that pattern
would need to be imposed by selectors. They seemed
to be the only ones who might reasonably have any
coherent notion of the role. Certainly, the time
and effort devoted to selection and the apparent
stringency of selection standards would seem to
support such a view. The three-day selection
procedure took the form of candidates completing a
variety of group and written exercises and each
being interviewed by the three selectors who made up
a panel. Selectors comprised a serving governor,
who acted as chairman, a member of the Prison
Psychological Service and an independent selector
provided by the Civil Service Selection Board,
usually a person of some eminence, retired from
public life and now familiar with selecting recruits
for other public bodies such as the police, fire
brigade and tax inspectorate. The selection ratio

was apparently quite stringent with only 32 of the 106 Open Competition candidates and 9 of the 72 Limited Competition candidates being successful, but more important perhaps was the fact that once selected, recruits faced no further selection process. The Staff College had for some years eschewed any secondary selection function on the grounds that it was unwise to make such a decision without the recruit's performance in the job itself having been assessed. Although the first two years are probationary and there is some 'wastage' during the period, there is no systematic attempt to reduce the overall number of recruits, which seems to imply a large measure of confidence in the selection criteria and procedure.

However, because of the diversity of the role, and the difficulties surrounding it, the selection process was not nearly so determinate as might appear. First, although the Prison Service provided a formal job specification outlining the requirements of the position, its content had changed during the preceding few years in line with the job advertisements mentioned earlier, from a primarily social casework emphasis to a managerial one. In 1972, the year in which these observations of the selection procedure were made, the job description had changed once more, giving further weight to the 'managerial' aspect of the role. Thus, all selectors were aware of the vacillation surrounding the definition of the role for which they were selecting candidates. In so far as they mentioned the formal job description at all, prison governors and psychologists tended to be critical or cynical of the increased managerial emphasis.

Second, at no time during the three separate panels that were observed was any mention, in fact, made of the formal job description. Indeed, the only explicit mention made of job requirements was when a candidate was rejected by a governor on the grounds that he would have 'trouble with casework'. What was evident, was that the CSSB procedure, that the Prison Service used in common with the police graduate entry scheme, senior fire brigade appointments and tax inspectorate, was exploited for its potential to reveal general personality characteristics of the candidates rather than specific, job-related aptitudes and abilities. Indeed, throughout the selection procedure there was an almost ostentatious avoidance of occupational relevance, tasks the candidate was asked to perform having no ostensible connection with the job for which he was being selected.

Third, whilst the actual selection criteria seemed to be defined in terms of general personality characteristics, these lacked clear definition. Much emphasis was laid upon 'presence' for instance, but this subjectively defined quality would appear to have been, in fact, applied somewhat contradic- torily, since on one occasion a candidate was rejected on the grounds that he had insufficient physique and, therefore, lacked 'presence', whereas others, of comparable physique, were selected despite this handicap.

Those recruited reflected the uncertainty of selection criteria since they were noticeably heterogenous in a wide variety of respects, some of which will be considered in greater detail in the next chapter. Suffice to say now that recruits, of whom four of the 33 were women, had a very wide age range, as can be seen from Figure 1.1, which at 23 years amounts almost to a generation. As might be expected, graduates were noticeably younger than either ex-officers or those direct-entrants who had changed their career, the mean ages being 23.64, 31.7, and 28.77 years respectively. Consistent with this wide age range, there were differences in marital status, with approximately two-thirds of recruits being married, of whom just over half, mainly ex-officers, had children. Of the remainder, eight were single and two divorced. Therefore, unlike others undergoing socialization, those entering the AG role were <u>not</u> also uniformly entering other life cycle roles in a way that would systematically affect the process.[66]

They were also distinctly heterogeneous with respect to social class, as can be seen from Table 1.1. Interestingly enough, direct-entrants show something of a U-curve distribution, tending to be either of higher or lower social status than ex- officers. Educational background too reflects marked diversity, with no ex-officer having stayed on at school either after the minimum school leaving age or having obtained GCE 'A' levels, whilst all direct-entrants had either a university degree or commensurate professional qualification.

Figure 1.1: Age Distribution of Recruits

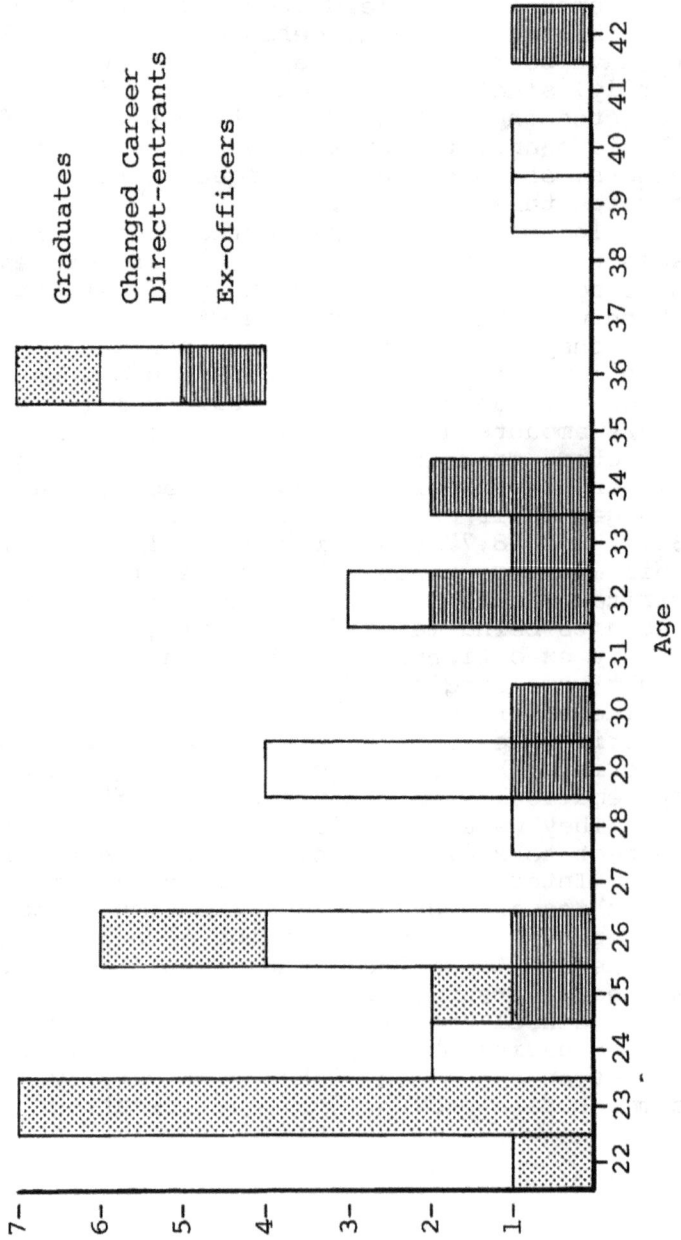

Table 1.1: Social Class Composition of AG Recruits

Socio-economic group:	Direct-entrants	Ex-officers	Total
Professionally qualified & high administrative	8	0	8
Managerial & executive	2	2	4
Inspectorial, supervisory & other non-manual	5	3	8
Routine non-manual & skilled manual	2	4	6
Manual semi-skilled	4	1	5
Manual routine	2	0	2

AGS: A SEVERE TEST OF SOCIALIZATION THEORY

Since socialization theoretically involves transforming a heterogeneous collection of people into a
homogeneous group, it follows that the more heterogeneous recruits are initially, the more demands are
placed upon the socialization process. Many occupations are quite successful in recruiting those
with common social characteristics, which thus
reduces the burden upon their subsequent socialization, for even if recruits share a common miscon-
ception about the occupation as, for example,
nursing students reportedly do in believing that
nursing is mainly devoted to the bedside care of
patients,[67] socializing agents at least know what
they have to deal with. When recruits are as
heterogeneous in their social characteristics as AGs
appear to be, agents are denied any coherent
conception of the 'typical' recruit.

However, if socialization theory is correct,
then we should expect that agents will make even
more strenuous attempts to ensure that socialization
is sufficient to mould even this diverse collection
of recruits into satisfactory members of the occupation, but it does mean that in this respect AGs
are a severe test of socialization theory.

The second respect in which AGs test the theory
is a more direct consequence of the background
conditions described above. The fact that the AG's
role is not uniform, and the problems of definition
which have afflicted it mean that those responsible
for socializing recruits are denied any clear

prescription upon which to base their training. Moreover, since the ambiguity and controversy surrounding the role has spread into the Staff College so as to maintain doubts about the proper function of training, the training staff were also uncertain about their role.

Again, however, although this means that AGs present socialization theory with a challenge, these conditions should not materially interfere with the adequate functioning of the socialization process. The theory emphasizes that it is not what agents consciously and explicitly do in the course of training that is most important for socialization, but the subtle, often unintended and unacknowledged, influences which they bring to bear, sometimes despite themselves, which have the most significant effects. The fact is that AGs continue to perform their ill-defined role despite these many difficulties, and those recruited as AGs continued to fill this position, which alone seems to indicate that socialization was, at least, minimally adequate - if the theory is to be believed.

RESEARCH DESIGN

In order to test whether a heterogeneous collection of individuals was transformed into a homogeneous group, as the theory predicts, a cohort of recruits was observed from shortly after their selection until the end of their training. This 'longitudinal' design is the most appropriate[68] to socialization research, since it enables us not only to assess aggregate attitudinal change, but also reveals how individuals have changed and whether these changes cancel each other out.

The difficulties with such a method are, first, that of time, for one needs to await the end of the socialization period before being able to analyse the patterns, and since the time available is usually limited, it means that a group can only be followed for a minimal period. It would, for example, have been useful to determine the different influences that working in a prison or borstal had upon AG recruits, but this would have led to an intolerable delay of several years before results could be analysed. Second, there is the problem that comes from repeatedly asking the same questions, in order to determine if there has been any change in attitudes, for in asking about various aspects of their socializing experiences, the researcher may

alert respondents to these very aspects and,
possibly, alter their susceptibility to such
influences. For this, and other reasons,[69] it is
preferable to record the attitudes of another group,
not undergoing socialization, who can then be used
as a baseline against which to compare any changes
of attitude amongst the researched group. Regret-
tably, resources were insufficient to employ a
control group in this manner. Nevertheless, despite
these problems the advantages of using a longitudinal design outweighed the disadvantages in
research of this kind.

As anticipatory socialization is a recognized
part of the wider socialization process,[70] recruits'
attitudes were determined at the earliest possible
opportunity. Other researchers have largely been
content to begin measuring attitudes upon the
recruits' entry to the training process, but it was
decided in this study to conduct the first interview
as soon after the recuits were notified of their
selection as could be arranged. It was important to
do this because ex-officers would receive some
preparatory academic and practical instruction at
their existing establishments and on occasional
visits to the Staff College before the course began,
and since also many direct-entrants took the opportunity to work as temporary prison officers during
the summer months preceding the start of the course.
Waiting until recruits arrived at the Staff College
to begin their training would have resulted in
missing their possibly important early experiences
of the new role. Therefore, all recruits were
visited in their homes or place of work as soon as
possible after they had been notified of their
recruitment. Since not all recruits were notified
at the same time, ex-officers having been selected
some weeks prior to direct-entrants, and since also
there was some inevitable delay in visiting recruits
scattered throughout the country, these interviews
could not be conducted at precisely the same time.
In only a very few cases, however, did this involve
any contamination in terms of the recruits' exposure
to any discernible socializing influences.

At the end of September, recruits spent two
weeks at the Staff College where they were given a
general introduction to the Service, the Staff
College and their role, before being attached to an
establishment for a period of three weeks. Ex-
officers and those direct-entrants who had worked as
temporary officers during the summer months were
sent to work alongside AGs, usually in an establish-

ment with which they were unfamiliar, whilst those direct-entrants without any experience of prison conditions, were sent to work as officers at local prisons near their homes. Since by their return to the Staff College, all recruits would have had at least some direct experience of prison reality, without yet receiving much in the way of formal training, standard tests were administered at that time and during the subsequent few weeks personal interviews were conducted.

The final interview took place in the last fortnight of the course, during the following May, when recruits knew to which establishments they were going, and in the last few days they again completed standard tests and questionnaires, in order to determine the outcome of the preceding socialization.

Participant Observation

Whilst standard tests and questionnaires might indicate the extent and direction of attitude change, they would tell us little about the sources of influence themselves. Should the socialization model prove inadequate, moreover, such information would not provide a sufficient basis for an alternative formulation. For these reasons it was decided to complement these measures with a participant observation of the day-to day experience of recruits.[71] Although this proved invaluable, it was not without its dangers, since in so far as one develops a suitable level of rapport for participant observation, this may affect answers given during interviews. This may occur in two ways: first, recruits might have been prepared to be more forthcoming in later interviews, when they were convinced that I was not part of the Prison Service hierarchy; but second, and more damagingly, they may have felt that some things could be taken for granted and left implicit in their replies to questions, leaving the researcher to interpret the meaning of these replies when coding the answers for tabular presentation. Again, it was thought that the benefits of participant observation outweighed these possible disadvantages, particularly since one advantage of combining participant observation and interviewing was that it would allow issues arising from the former to be pursued in the latter.

Measuring Attitude Change

The guiding principle in deciding upon which specific techniques to use, was that they should appertain directly to the specific role for which AGs were ostensibly being socialized. Frequently in socialization research, it seems that scales are employed mainly because of their availability rather than because they relate directly to the group under consideration. There may be good reasons for the use of tests, such as authoritarianism on such occupations as the police,[72] but too often the justific--ation for selecting this variable as opposed to others is left unstated.

On the other hand, this approach created problems, because it was quickly discovered that there were few, if any, standardized attitude scales that were specific to prison staff, still less AGs. There was just one exception, a scale designed to reveal the evaluation of the criminal justice system devised by Walter Reckless,[73] and standardized on an international sample of prison staff, police officers and probation officers, as well as laymen and prisoners. Useful though this was, it was hardly sufficient for determining the extent and direction of socializing influences.

S   Semi-structured interviewing could fill some of the gap, having the benefit of flexibility that comes from the focused interview[74] whilst retaining some of the rigour that comes from standardized questions. It was decided to adopt the method of 'funnelling'[75] questions, which involves asking highly general questions designed to avoid imposing the researcher's frame of reference upon the respondent, before going on to explore some of the more specific issues in which the researcher is interested. However, the problem with such techniques is the coding and tabulation of replies, which necessarily involves a considerable degree of interpretation. Safeguards can be employed to mitigate this as much as possible, such as dividing the sample randomly in half, so that one half can be scrutinized to produce an exhaustive set of categories which can then be applied to the other. Nevertheless, such a method cannot be as rigorously standardized as can others.

If there were to be some specific measures of the extent and direction of change in attitudes directly related to the AG's future occupation, then there were just two alternatives, either construct-ing an attitude scale for the purpose of this research or using semi-structured techniques. The first alternative would have been a considerable undertaking, even if resources had been available, and in addition there would have been considerable difficulties in piloting such a scale[76] without, at the same time, contaminating the research by alerting possible socializing agents amongst the small number of governor grades as to its aims. Knowing what attitudes the researcher was interested in, AGs who had cooperated in the pilot studies may have adjusted their behaviour towards the recruits and, thereby, the kind of influence they may have been able to exert. It was, therefore, decided that a semi-structured technique was most appropriate, especially one capable of statistical analysis.

The technique chosen was that of the repertory grid,[77] because apart from various purely technical advantages, it has one major advantage for socialization research – it not only detects changes in the perception of items, but also the changing relevance of the perceptual categories themselves. To explain, it is normally the case that a researcher specifies the attitude scales in terms of which change will be measured throughout the socializing period. Thus, recruits would be asked to complete scales on a number of predetermined occasions and their scores compared over time as a measure of change. However, such a procedure assumes that the scale itself has the same continuing relevance throughout the period, but this need not be the case at all. The Reckless scale, for example, measured AG recruits' evaluation of the criminal justice system, but there was no guarantee that recruits actually saw the prison system as part of that wider system, say, at the beginning of their training, whereas they may have been acutely aware of this relationship at the end. However, all that would have been measured were recruits' evaluations, and these may not even have changed.

The repertory grid does not make this assumption, since it allows the respondent to employ scales which are relevant to him at the time of completing the test. This is achieved through the 'triadic sort' procedure: the respondent takes three of the items from the list at random and is asked to say what important characteristic two items have in common and which is not shared by the third. All the items are then rated or ranked in terms of that characteristic, which forms the scale. This, therefore, allows recruits to include or introduce those scales which seem relevant at one stage of their socialization, whilst omitting them at other stages when they no longer seem relevant. It is, therefore, possible to detect not only how the rating of items alters during socialization, but also how perceptual relevancies change.

The technique also has the considerable advantage, particularly where pilot studies are severely circumscribed, of limiting the extent to which the researcher can impose his frame of reference upon the respondent. Clearly, the researcher does, usually, specify the elements to be rated or ranked, but he does not predetermine the categories in terms of which this must be done.

However, the danger is that such a technique will simply produce an assortment of idiosyncratic judgements, unsuitable to the analysis of social processes. This can be overcome by including a number of additional scales predetermined by the researcher and which remain constant throughout the period, but are completed only after the respondent has produced his own scales through the 'triadic sort'. These 'supplied constructs' can then be intercorrelated with the respondent's own 'elicited constructs' in order to determine their relevance to him.

Thus, for each respondent there will be a number of elements assessed in terms of a series of scales repeated on several occasions. The advantage of this is the obvious richness of the data that is collected, but the attendant difficulty lies in analysing such a wealth of information. One solution is to submit all this data to statistical analyses which are designed to order and simplify it, the most commonly used being that of the Ingrid principal components analysis developed specifically for this purpose by Patrick Slater.[78]

What Ingrid does is to express for each individual on each separate occasion the relationship between elements, constructs, and elements and constructs, in a common 'space'. This 'space' is produced by extracting, statistically, the underlying dimensions within the data, in such a way that the first dimension accounts for the greatest proportion of the variance in the raw data matrix, and so on until all the variance is accounted for. Usually, researchers are interested only in the first two or three dimensions, since these normally account for the vast majority of the total variance and can be usefully conceptualized as a physical space within which elements and constructs are located.

In order to obtain the enormous benefits of

Such an analysis it is necessary to make a series of assumptions about the way in which individuals construe their experiences which amount to believing that they do so with mathematical logic. Only in this way is it possible to reproduce their perceptions through this statistical device. Clearly, such an assumption is at best an unwarranted leap of faith and it would seem prudent not to rely wholly upon it. Moreover, since each individual's repertory grid would need to be analysed separately, it would be advantageous if any patterns discerned could be independently tested.

The solution adopted was to treat the Ingrid analysis as a heuristic device which could assist in producing working hypotheses, which could then be independently tested through other statistical techniques. Thus, each individual grid completed on each occasion was mapped in a two dimensional space, relationships between elements and constructs were noted and then independently subjected to tests of statistical significance. The analysis of variance employed for this purpose, used recruits' original ratings as data, thereby avoiding the need to 'normalize'[79] individual scores, and for each construct determined whether recruits' constructions of each element were statistically significantly different, and also whether they rated all elements more or less the same, or differently.

There remained only one major problem in using the repertory grid technique and this lay in its administration. The first time a respondent was asked to complete it was in the course of an extended interview in his home or place of work, when in a person-to-person interview, he could be assisted through the test. However, to repeat such a test when recruits had begun their training would certainly have taken a number of days and possibly weeks, during which time they may have been subjected to socializing influences which meant that not all the test results would be equivalent. Therefore, it was necessary to administer the test en masse and a booklet was devised which required respondents to complete a triadic sort and then rate all the elements in terms of the constructs thus generated.[80] However, what this method of self-administration did expose was the difficulty of using bi-polar as opposed to uni-polar constructs.

Normally, the aim of the triadic sort is to encourage the respondent to produce not only the characteristic that two of the elements have in common, but also the characteristic that sets the third apart. The reason for this is that one person may distinguish 'tough' from 'weak' whereas another may distinguish 'tough' from 'sensitive', for example. To ask respondents simply to rate or rank elements in terms of their 'toughness' would not reflect the differences of meaning that this construct had for these two hypothetical respondents. Unfortunately, they might reply to the triadic sort by giving an untrue contrast, such as 'tough'-'intelligent', which they recognise to be a mistake once the researcher asks them if the one construct is the opposite of the other. If, however, a repertory grid is to be self-administered there is no opportunity for the researcher to probe apparently questionable distinctions of this sort and uni-polar constructs have, therefore, to be used with the loss of subtlety in interpreting the meaning of constructs that this entails.

One minor consequence of using self-administered grids, was that in the time made available for this exercise, it was not possible to elicit as many constructs as under conditions of a personal interview. The loss of richness in the information yielded, though regrettable, was a small price to pay compared to the opportunity to measure recruits' attitude at a given moment of their training.

SUMMARY AND CONCLUSIONS

This research set out to test orthodox socialization theory as it is applied to occupations. That theory proposes that when recruits enter an occupation they are moulded by agents, preferably in a residential training organization, so as to accept and conform to the expectations, formal and informal, of their role.

Although AGs satisfy the requirements of such a model, there are good, albeit commonsense, reasons for supposing that socialization may not be as effective in their case. First, the role of AG is obscure to many of the recruits, especially those entering from outside the Prison Service. In addition, it has been historically both confused and surrounded by controversy within the Prison Service, so that there are doubts as to the appropriate expectations of the role. Third, there are similar doubts surrounding the Staff College and AGs Course, which have left the justification for the training of AGs somewhat questionable, both in terms of content and structure. There had been considerable uncertainty about whether the course should be a social casework training or course or a management course, and its aspirations to the quasi-professional application of social science theory to penal practice were also placed in doubt by the inability of the social sciences to provide definitive, relevant knowledge.

Despite these evident difficulties, the social-ization of AGs should be effective, if orthodox theory is correct, since AGs do actually perform their diverse duties in various establishments throughout the prison system. This, they could not do, if they had not been adequately socialized.

To test whether or not the heterogeneous collection of individuals who were recruited as AGs was transformed into a homogeneous social group by their initial training, a particular cohort of recruits was observed from shortly after their selection until the end of their training. Using a variety of techniques, recruits attitudes towards their future role and wider context were measured on three occasions thoughout their training; shortly after selection, at the beginning of formal instruction, and at the end of the training course. In addition to this, a participant observation was conducted during the period recruits were at the Staff College to obtain some qualitative under-standing of how they experienced the socialization process. This was undertaken in order to provide an empirical basis for suggesting a modification or alternative to orthodox socialization theory.

NOTES

1. Perhaps the clearest and most authoritative expression of this preoccupation is in the work of Emile Durkheim who emphasized the moral integration of society and feared for its breakdown in contem-porary industrial societies. See, E. Durkheim, Suicide, translated by J.A. Spaulding and G. Simpson (London, Routledge, 1952) and also his Sociology and Philosophy, translated by D.F. Pocock (New York, Free Press, 1974).

2. The clearest statements of such views of socialization are often to be found in standard textbooks on sociology, such as K. Davis, Human Society (New York, Macmillan, 1949); H.C. Bredemeir and R.M. Stephenson, The Analysis of Social Systems (New York, Holt, 1962); and R. Beirstedt, The Social Order (2nd edn., New York, McGraw-Hill, 1963).

Basic sources devoted exclusively to socialization theory include: O.G. Brim and S. Wheeler, Socialization After Childhood: Two Essays (New York, Wiley, 1966); J.A. Clausen, 'Introduction' in J.A. Clausen (ed), Socialization and Society (Boston, Little Brown, 1968); D.A. Goslin (ed), Handbook of Socialization Theory and Research (Chicago, Rand McNally, 1969), especially the introduction and contributions by A. Inkeles, 'Social Structure and Socialization' and W.E. Moore, 'Occupational Socialization'; the introduction to D. Heise (ed), Personality and Socialization (Chicago, Rand McNally, 1972); E.Q. Campbell, 'The Internalization of Moral Norms', Sociometry, 1964, vol. 27 (4), pp 391-412; E. McNeil, Human Socialization (Belmont, California, Brooks Cole, 1969).

3. See: O.G. Brim, 'Adult Socialization' in J.A. Clausen (ed), op cit; W.E. Moore, op cit; V. Olesen and E.E. Whittaker, The Silent Dialogue (San Francisco, Jossey Bass, 1968); I.H. Simpson, From Student to Nurse (Cambridge University Press, 1979); S. Wheeler, 'The Structure of Formally Organized Socialization Settings' in Brim and Wheeler, op cit.

4. R. Benedict, Patterns of Culture (Boston, Houghton-Mifflin, 1934).

5. R.K. Merton, 'Socialization: a Terminological Note' in R.K. Merton, G.G. Reader and P.L. Kendall, The Student Physician (Cambridge, Massachusetts, Harvard University Press, 1957, p 287).

6. S. Lieberman, 'Some Effects of Change in Role on Role Occupants', Human Relations, 1956, vol. 9 (4), pp 385-403.

7. Davis, op cit, p 129.

8. Brim, in Brim and Wheeler, op cit, p 4.

9. Clausen, op cit, pp 9-10.

10. R. Fox, 'Training for Uncertainty' in Merton, et al, op cit.

11. Davis, op cit, pp 401-04.

12. R. Dawson and K. Prewitt, Political Socialization (Boston, Little Brown, 1969); D. Easton and J. Dennis, Children in the Political System (New York, McGraw-Hill, 1969); H. Hyman, Political Socialization (New York, Free Press, 1959); L. Pye, Politics, Personality and Nation Building (New Haven, York University Press, 1962); B. Stacey, Political Socialization in Western Democracies (London, Arnold, 1978).

13. Clausen, op cit, p 7.

14. E. Jones and H. Gerard, Foundations of

Social Psychology (New York, Wiley, 1967, pp 85-6).

15. S.M. Dornbusch, 'The Military Academy as an Assimilating Institutions', Social Forces, vol. 33 (2), 1955, pp 316-21.

16. J. Lovell, 'The Professional Socialization of the West Point Cadet' in M. Janowitz (ed), The New Military (New York, Sage, 1964); G. Wamsley, 'Contrasting Institutions of Air Force Socialization: Happenstance or Bellwether?', American Journal of Sociology, 1972, vol. 78 (2), pp 399-417; L. Zurcher, 'The Naval Recruit Training Centre: a Study of Role Socialization in a Total Institution', Sociological Inquiry, 1967, vol. 37 (Winter), pp 85-95.

17. Op cit.

18. D. Wrong, 'The Over-Socialized Conception of Man in Modern Sociology', American Sociological Review, vol. 26 (2), 1961, pp 184-93.

19. Other critics include: D. Atkinson, Orthodox Consensus and Radical Alternative (London, Heinemann, 1971); A. Dawe, 'The Two Sociologies', British Journal Sociology, 1970, vol. 21 (2), pp 207-18; D. Easton, 'The Theoretical Relevance of Political Socialization', Canadian Journal of Political Science, 1968, vol. 1 (2), pp 124-46; A.W. Gouldner, The Coming Crisis in Western Sociology (London, Heinemann, 1970, ch.   ); D. Lockwood, 'Social Integration and System Integration' in G. Zollschan and W. Hirsch (eds), Explorations in Social Change (London, Routledge, 1964).

20. See, for example: I. Adler and J.T. Shuval, 'Cross Pressures During Socialization for Medicine', American Sociological Review, 1978, vol. 43 (5), pp 693-704; J.T. Shuval and I. Adler, 'Health Occupations in Isreal: Comparative Patterns of Change During Socialization', Journal of Health and Social Behaviour, 1979, vol. 20 (March), pp 77-89; W. Arkin and L.R. Dobrofsky, 'Military Socialization and Masculinity', Journal of Social Issues, 1978, vol. 34 (1), pp 151-68; H.S. Erlanger and D.A. Klegon, 'Socialization Effects of Professional School: the Law School Experience and Student Orientations to Public Interest Concerns', Law and Social Review, 1978, vol. 13 (1), pp 11-35; M. Hopper, 'Becoming a Policeman: Socialization of Cadets in a Police Academy', Urban Life, 1977, vol. 6 (2), pp 149-70; C.F. Shatan, 'Bogus Manhood, Bogus Honour: Surrender and Transfiguration in the U.S. Marine Corps', Psychoanalytic Review, 1977, vol. 64 (4), pp 585-610; P.B. Wild, 'Social Origins and Ideology of Chiropractors: an Empirical Study of

the Socialization of the Chiropractic Student',
Sociological Symposium, 1978, vol. 27 (Spring),
pp 33-54.

21. I. Simpson, op cit.

22. See: H.S. Becker, et al, Boys in White
(Chicago University Press, 1961); R. Dingwall, The
Social Organisation of Health Visitor Training
(London, Croom Helm, 1978); C. Lacey, The
Socialization of teachers (London, Methuen, 1977);
and Olesen and Whittaker, op cit.

23. The sociological literature on occupations
is replete with examples of this, but one of the
clearest examples is Fox, op cit.

24. In some respects the organization and
structure of the Prison Service has changed since
this research was completed, for example, there is
no longer a sharp distinction between male and
female Services so far as governor grades are
concerned. This description relates to the situation as it was during the early-to-middle 1970s
when this research was undertaken.

25. Home Office, Report on the Work of the
Prison Department, 1974.

26. The 'wings' of a prison are the main blocks
of cellular accommodation, which, in the most
traditional, Victorian prison designs, radiate from
the central hub. The modern prisons no longer have
this radial pattern, but still designate accommodation blocks as 'wings'. In Scotland cell blocks
are known as 'halls'.

'Houses' are the borstal equivalent of 'wings',
the term being derived from the English Public
Schools, upon which borstals were modelled.

27. Wheeler, op cit.

28. Op cit.

29. I.H. Simpson, 'Patterns of Socialization
Into Professions: the Case of the Student Nurse',
Sociological Inquiry, 1967, vol. 37 (1), pp 47-54.

30. M.J. Huntingdon, 'The Development of a
Professional Self-Image' in Merton, et al, op cit.

31. For a history of the prison system and the
development of the governor grades, see J.E. Thomas,
The English Prison Officer Since 1850 (London,
Routledge, 1972).

32. Editorial, Prison Service Journal, 1972,
no. 7, p 18.

33. Advisory Council on the Treatment of
Offenders, The Organization of After-Care, H.M.S.O.,
1969, pp 26-7.

34. B. Marchant, 'What is a Housemaster?',
Prison Service Journal, 1965, vol. 4, no. 15,

pp 44-5.

35. Sir Lionel Fox, The Modern English Prison (London, Routledge, 1934).

36. Sir Lionel Fox, The English Prison and Borstal Service (London, Routledge, 1952).

37. Governors' Branch of the Society Civil Servants, Memorandum on Management Structure and Organization in Prison Departments, submitted to Management Review Committee, p 7.

38. People in Prison (H.M.S.O., Cmmd. 4214, 1969) gave priority to containment before rehabilitation in describing the aims of the Service, see p 7, para. 13.

39. Although it is widely accepted throughout the Prison Service, and often cited by commentators, that the reconviction rate for borstal trainees is 70-80 per cent after two years, little accurate information is available to confirm this. The problem arises because borstal sentences are not considered as previous prison sentences amongst adult prisoners and do not, therefore, emerge from the statistics on imprisonment. The most accurate figures were published in Prisons and Borstals (H.M.S.O., 1960), which showed that over a seven year follow-up period, reconvictions had risen from 19,5 per cent in 1937-8, to 26.3 per cent in 1952-4, and that by 1957-8 the number of reconvictions had risen to 29.3 per cent during a two-year follow-up period. For an example of contemporary, official concern at the failure of the borstal system, see Advisory Council on the Penal System, 'Young Adult Offenders' (The Younger Report), H.M.S.O., 1974.

40. In academic criminology the 'return to justice' movement has drawn attention to the dangers inherent in the rehabilitative ethic which necessarily vests authority for making penal decisions in the hands of the executive. For example, the Parole Board makes decisions regarding the continued custody of offenders without the prisoner or his legal representative present and without giving the grounds upon which the decision is made.

41. D. Sherwood, 'Prison as a Last Resort', Prison Service Journal, 1972, no. 5, pp 8-9. See also, M. Selby's letter to the editor, Prison Service Journal, 1971, no. 4, p 18.

42. Governors' Branch, Society of Civil Servants, evidence to the 11th Report of the Estimates Committee - Prisons, Borstals and Detention Centres, 1967.

43. D. Hewlings, 'The Role of the Assistant Governor', and D. Gould, 'The Role of the Assistant

Governor', both papers read to the South Region, AGs' Conference, 1968, unpublished report, p 34 and p 43.

44. See: J. Lee, Managing to Govern', <u>Prison Service Journal</u>, 1966, vol. 5, pp 8-18; G. Dowell, 'Inside Management', <u>Prison Service Journal</u>, 1967, vol. 6, pp 27-31; G. Hart, 'The Administration Officer', <u>Prison Service Journal</u>, 1967, vol. 6, pp 32-35; J. Clarke, letter to the editor, <u>Prison Service Journal</u>, 1967, vol. 6, pp 36-37; T. Carnegie, 'Borstal and After-Care - Post ACTO', <u>Prison Service Journal</u>, 1966, vol. 5, pp 44-48.

45. Mr. R.S. Llewellyn, then Chairman of the Governors' Branch, Society of Civil Servants, open letter to the Director General of the Prison Service, 1973; 27th AGs Course project report, 'Lay Out Requirements for Initial Assistant Governor Training', Staff College, 1971.

46. Advisory Council on the Treatment of Offenders, op cit.

47. Op cit.

48. P.S. Lewis, 'Custody and Treatment', <u>Prison Service Journal</u>, 1966, vol. 5, pp 44-48; P. Lowry, 'The English Prison Welfare Service', <u>International Journal of Offender Therapy and Comparative Criminology</u>, 1972, vol. 17 (3), pp 29-40; P. Priestly, 'The Prison Welfare Officer - a Case of Role Strain', <u>British Journal of Sociology</u>, 1972, vol. 17 (3), pp 221-35; H. Klare, <u>Anatomy of Prison</u> (Harmondsworth, Penguin, 1966, p 51).

49. The Younger Report, op cit.

50. One of the most recent, and which was eagerly awaited at the time this research was being conducted, was the 'Report and Recommendations of the Third Stage Management Review', 1975, unpublished memorandum.

51. See: Lee, op cit; Dowell, op cit; Hart, op cit; Clarke, op cit.

52. 4-14th Staff Course reports, unpublished.

53. Op cit.

54. 22nd AGs Course report, unpublished.

55. The status of the Management Studies course changed during the period of the fieldwork, from being taught by AG tutors in the Staff College, to being taught by visiting lecturers from the Manchester Business School.

56. 22nd AGs Course report, op cit.

57. The revised AGs Course was first introduced in 1973.

58. The traits approach is most clearly defined by E. Greenwood, 'The Elements of Professionaliz-

ation', in H. Vollmer and D. Mills (eds),
Professionalization (Englewood Cliffs, Prentice Hall,
1966). See also: A. Etzioni, The Semi-Professions
and Their Organization (New York, Free Press, 1969)
and H. Wilensky, 'The Professionalization of
Everyone?', American Journal of Sociology, 1964,
vol. 70 (2), pp 137-57. Critics of this approach
include: P. Elliott, The Sociology of the
Professions (London, Macmillan, 1972); T. Johnson,
Professions and Power (London, Macmillan, 1972);
C. Turner and M. Hodge, 'Occupations and Professions'
in J. Jackson (ed), Professions and Professionalization (Cambridge University Press, 1970); and
R. Bucher and A. Strauss, 'Professions in Process',
American Journal of Sociology, 1961, vol. 66 (4),
pp 325-34.
    59. This argument is developed further in
P.A.J. Waddington, 'The Professional Training of
Governor Grades?' (unpublished paper read to the
northern region meeting of the Institute for the
Study and Treatment of Delinquency, Febuary, 1974)
    60. Wilensky, op cit, p 145.
    61. W.J. Goode, 'Encroachment, Charlatanism and
the Emerging Professions', American Sociological
Review, 1960, vol. 25 (6), pp 902-14.
    62. Central Council for Education and Training
in Social Work, The Teaching of Sociology in Social
Work Courses (Discussion Document, No. 5, 1968,
London, p 10).
    63. P.A.J. Waddington, 'Indeterminacy in
Occupational Recruitment: the Case of Prison
Assistant Governors', Sociology, 1982, vol. 18 (2),
pp 203-19.
    64. See: E. Ginsberg, S. Ginsberg, S. Axelrod
and J. Herma, Occupational Choice: An Approach to a
General Theory (New York, Columbia, 1951); D. Super,
'A Theory of Vocational Development', American
Psychologist, 1953, vol. 8 (5), pp 185-90; J. Ford
and S. Box, 'Sociological Theory and Occupational
Choice', Sociological Review, 1967, vol. 15 (3),
pp 287-99; P.W. Musgrave, 'Towards a Sociological
Theory of Occupational Choice', Sociological Review,
1967, vol. 15 (1), pp 33-46; and D.N. Ashton, 'The
Transition from School to Work', Sociological Review,
1973, vol. 21 (1), pp 101-25.
    65. For further details see, P.A.J. Waddington,
The Occupational Socialization of Prison Governors
(unpublished Ph.D. thesis, University of Leeds,
1977).
    66. F. Davis and V.L. Olesen, 'Initiation into
a Women's Profession: Identity Problems in the

Status Transition of Coed to Student Nurse',
Sociometry, 1963, vol. 26 (1), pp 89-101.

67. Simpson, *From Student to Nurse*, op cit.

68. P.F. Lazarsfeld, B. Berelson and H. Gaudet,
The People's Choice (New York, Columbia, 1948);
P.F. Lazarsfeld, 'The Use of Panels in Social
Research', *Proceedings of the American Philosophical
Society*, 1948, vol. 42 (5), pp 405-10; C. Glock,
'Some Applications of the Panel Method to the Study
of Change' in P.F. Lazarsfeld and M. Rosenberg (eds),
The Language of Social Research (New York, Free
Press, 1955).

69. The main reason control groups are employed
in research is to detect any source of attitude
change external to the socializing organization
itself. Apart from the riots at a number of prisons
during the summer months preceding the course, there
was no reason to believe that there were any other
external factors influencing attitudes.

70. R.F. Merton, *Social Theory and Social
Structure* (Glencoe, Free Press, 1957, pp 265-8).

71. For further discussion see Waddington,
thesis, op cit, ch. 7. See also, H.S. Becker and
B. Geer, 'Participant Observation and Interviewing:
a Comparison', *Human Organization*, 1957, vol. 16 (3),
pp 28-32; N.K. Denzin, *The Research Act in Sociology*
(London, Butterworth, 1970); C. Selltiz, M. Jahoda,
M. Deutsch and S. Cook, *Research Methods in Social
Relations* (London, Methuen, 1965, ch. 6); H.S.
Becker, 'Problems of Inference and Proof in
Participant Observation', *American Sociological
Review*, 1958, vol. 23 (6), pp 652-60; G. McCall and
J. Simmons (eds), *Issues in Participant Observation*
(Reading, Massachusetts, Addison-Wesley, 1969);
R. Gold, 'Roles in Sociological Field Observations',
Social Forces, 1958, vol. 36 (3), pp 217-23.

72. I. Guller, 'Higher Education and Policemen:
Attitudinal Differences Between Freshmen and Senior
Police College Students', *Journal of Criminal Law,
Criminology and Police Science*, 1972, vol. 63 (3),
pp 396-401.

73. A. Mylonas and W. Reckless, 'Prisoner's
Attitudes Towards Law and Legal Institutions',
*Journal of Criminal Law, Criminology and Police
Science*, 1963, vol. 54 (4), pp 479-84.

74. For an account of the focused interview
technique, see: C. Cannell and R. Kahn, 'The
Collection of Data by Interviewing' in L. Festinger
and D. Katz (eds), *Research Methods in the
Behavioural Sciences* (New York, Dryden, 1953);
W.J. Goode and P. Hatt, *Methods in Social Research*

(New York, McGraw-Hill, 1952, ch. 13); and Selltiz, et al, op cit, ch. 7.

75. 'Funnelling' is explained further in A. Oppenheim, Questionnaire Design and Attitude Measurement (London, Heinemann, 1966, pp 38-40).

76. In order to construct an attitude scale, it would have been necessary to test items for validity and reliability upon serving AGs before the test was applied to recruits.

77. For a further account of the repertory grid technique and discussion, see: D. Bannister and J. Mair, The Evaluation of Personal Constructs (London, Academic, 1968); and F. Fransella and D. Bannister, A Manual of Repertory Grid Techniques (London, Academic, 1977).

78. P. Slater, Notes on Ingrid 72, a Handbook for the Users of the Ingrid Programme (Institute of Psychiatry, Denmark Hill, London, 1972). See also, P. Slater, The Measurement of Intrapersonal Space by Grid Technique (vols. 1 & 2, London, Wiley, 1976).

79. 'Normalized' constructs are 'rescaled so that they each have their total variance put equal to unity' (Slater, Notes on Ingrid 72, op cit)

80. Respondents were instructed as follows: If the characteristic is wholly applicable to the particular group, score '+2'; if only partially applicable, score '+1'. If, on the other hand, it is definitely not applicable, score '-2', and if only partially inapplicable, score '-1'. If you do not know, or the characteristic is entirely irrelevant to the group in question, or if for any reason you cannot answer, score '0'.

Chapter Two

IDENTIFICATION AND IDEALISM: PATTERNS OF ATTITUDE
CHANGE AMONGST AGs

INTRODUCTION

Socialization theory maintains that upon entering an
occupation, a heterogeneous collection of individuals will be transformed into a functionally homogeneous group. Therefore, we would expect that
during the period of their induction into the
governor grades, AGs would become increasingly alike
in their work-related attitudes.

There is a problem in attempting to test such a
hypothesis, for, on the one hand, it is necessary to
measure those attitudes which are functionally
relevant to the occupation, whilst on the other,
avoiding attitudes which are wholly idiosyncratic to
those employed in a particular job. Idiosyncracy
may reflect occupational relevance directly, but
will prevent comparison with socialization for other
occupations. However, comparability can be bought
at the expense of functional relevance when, for
example, patterns of change in authoritarianism are
measured in occupations which have no apparent
functional need for the authoritarian personality.

In attempting to reconcile these two considerations, attitudes were selected for investigation
which were general enough for comparisons to be
drawn with other occupations, but were capable of
being operationalized so as to reflect the idiosyncracies of the AG's role. The first attitude was
that of 'identification with the role' which is
generally thought by socialization theorists to be
both high and to increase further during socialization, although it should be noted that how this is
exhibited will depend upon the particular characteristics of the role with which they identify.

The second attitude selected for investigation
was that of idealism, about which theorists

are less agreed as to its expected pattern of change. Like identification, this attitude allows us to draw broad comparisons between different occupations, whilst allowing particularities about each to be reflected in the way it is measured. Each occupation gives its members different things to be idealistic or cynical about.

IDENTIFICATION

It can hardly be doubted that identification with the future role is thought to be important in socialization, since it is through this means that particular norms, values and attitudes are believed to be internalized. This is so, no less for recruits identification with their new occupational role, as it is for the child's identification with its parent.[1]

However, despite the undoubted importance of the process, the meaning of the term 'identification' has remained rather confused. It would appear that, in fact, it is used in three, closely connected, though analytically separable ways:

1. It refers to a cognitive process, in the sense in which a witness might be asked to identify a suspect, that is, it is an act of recognition. In social relations, it is not the physical appearance of a person that matters so much, but whether they are recognized in terms of salient social categories, such as whether they are 'intelligent', 'hospitable', 'lonely' and so forth. Since it is possible to identify persons in terms of a series of such salient social characteristics, it is also possible to compare different persons according to the extent to which they share such characteristics. This comparison may, of course, include the person making it, that is, estimating how much or little he has in common with some other or others.

2. There is the emotional bond that is often implied in the term 'identification'. This refers to the desire by the person making a comparison between himself and another to be as much like that other person as possible. Although this is normally thought of as a positive process it need not be, since the person could equally desire to share as little in common with another as possible or even to acquire the opposite characteristics to those perceived in the other person.

3. There is the behavioural consequence of the desire to become like another, expressed through

imitation, emulation, role-modelling and attachment, in which the person seeks to acquire those social characteristics possessed by that other person. It is this, of course, which is crucial for socialization.

Normally, identification involves other people, but it is not necessary that it should, since the person could identify with any personalized object to which social characteristics could be attributed, such as legendary figures, ancestors, or an occupational role-image. For example, it is argued that when a medical student adopts a 'clinical attitude' of emotional distance from the patient, he is trying to be the type of person a doctor is. He has identified these behavioural characteristics cognitively, desires to be like other doctors and so behaves accordingly.

Thus, at the most general level, socialization theory proposes that identification with the new role will be high throughout and increase during socialization, as the person comes to recognise more characteristics associated with the role. More specifically, although socialization theorists are not at all precise about identification, it would seem that identification is characterised by:

1. The new role being dominant in the recruits' perceptions so that recruits come to see all roles in terms of its distinguishing characteristics.
2. The new role becoming, increasingly, to be seen as exclusive, that is, distinctive in its characteristics from all others.
3. Recruits increasingly identifying themselves with the role as they perceive themselves acquiring its distinguishing social characteristics.
4. Recruits constantly desiring to become like the role image.

To see whether this was true of AGs, we must now turn to the empirical data, first the repertory grid analysis and then the interviews.

The Repertory Grid Analysis

The repertory grid technique is particularly suitable for the investigation of patterns of identification – at least in its cognitive and emotional aspects – because the person is required to provide a series of characteristics and to compare given social roles, including their future role, in these terms, and this furnishes us with the raw data for

identification processes. Furthermore, the
principal component analysis not only allows us to
inspect the degree of intercorrelation between
different roles, but also orders the whole matrix so
as to suggest which characteristics are most
salient.[2] By including the two supplied constructs,
'Like I am now' and 'Like I would like to be', it is
possible to investigate the emotional dimension of
identification.

The grid used in this research contained twelve
role titles associated with the Prison Service,[3]
which, it was hoped, would reflect the various
aspects of prison work. These included the three
governor grade titles, 'governor', 'assistant
governor in a prison', and 'borstal housemaster'.
Representing the uniformed, discipline grades were
the titles 'basic grade discipline officer' and
'chief officer'. Specialist roles included were
'chaplain', 'education officer', 'prison welfare
officer', 'medical officer' and 'administration
officer'. 'Member of the board of visitors' was
included to represent the wider context of the
prison system, because this body acts both in a
disciplinary capacity and as a public watchdog.
Finally, and most controversially,[4] the 'police
officer' was included, not because AGs have very
much direct contact with the police, but because the
police represent the wider criminal justice system,
through their contact with the prisoner before he
arrives in prison or borstal, and they also have an
interest in prison security.

In addition to the elicited constructs that
recruits provided, each was given eight supplied
constructs which would form a common set for
comparative purposes.[5] These supplied constructs
included 'Like I am now' and 'Like I would like to
be', mentioned above, but also other constructs
designed to reveal other aspects of identification.
Four of these constructs referred to debates
regarding the AG's role. 'Managers' was designed to
see if recruits saw governor grades in terms of the
'managerial' definition of the role, as opposed to
'care about inmates' which was designed to tap the
more caring social casework view of the role with
its concern for individual inmates rather than the
institution. Whilst 'rehabilitate inmates' and
'discipline' were designed to reveal recruits'
perceptions of their future role in relation to the
perennial 'treatment versus custody' debate. The
final two constructs being 'have high standing in
the prison' and 'do the _real_ job in prison' which

were evaluative in character.

After this grid was administered to recruits, principal components analysis revealed a pattern common amongst recruits and which stayed more or less constant throughout the socializing period. The salient characteristics of these grids were, first, that discipline staff, specialists and governor grades all formed distinct clusters. Second, that the uniformed staff and specialists were each associated with particular constructs which indicated a polarization between custody and welfare. Third, that the majority of constructs clustered around the three governor grades with little distinction between them, indicating the perceived concern of governors and AGs with the whole establishment rather than any particular aspect or function of it. Fourth, the police officer was isolated from all the other roles with few, if any, constructs associated with it. Finally, the grids were simple, as indicated by the fact that the first two components accounted for two-thirds of the total variance.

Once these impression had been gained from visual inspection, the grids were subjected to a three-factor analysis of variance.[6] This would inevitably be limited to the supplied constructs only, since these were the only constructs common to all recruits and were repeated on every occasion the test was administered. The additional use of the studentized range statistic revealed the patterns of statistical association and difference between the various roles on each supplied construct and on each occasion.[7]

As anticipated, 'rehabilitate inmates' and 'discipline' distinguished uniformed grades from specialists as shown in Figures 2.1 and 2.2. The construct 'discipline' shows a distinct division of labour which hardly changes throughout the period. 'Discipline' is most explicitly the province of the two uniformed grades, with all the specialists significantly dissociated from this function. The construct 'rehabilitate inmates' does not show such a clear composition but exhibits distinct signs of the reverse pattern, especially initially, when all the specialists, except the medical officer, were closely associated with the construct, whilst both uniformed grades were not. The overall pattern remains largely unchanged, apart from the noticeable way in which the discipline officer is detached from the chief officer and seen to play an increasing part in the rehabilitation function.

Figure 2.1: Means and Studentized Clusters for Elements on the Construct 'Rehabilitate Inmates.

Occasion I –

Police	AO		MO	Chief	Offr	BoV		EdO	Govr	Chap	AG	Hm	PWO
1.2	1.2		2.1	2.2	2.5	2.6		3.6	3.6	3.7	3.9	4.2	4.2

Occasion II –

Police	AO		Chief	MO		BoV		Govr	Offr		Chap	G	EdO		PWO	Hm
1.3	1.4		2.0	2.4		2.6		3.7	3.8		3.9	4.0	4.0		4.5	4.6

Occasion III –

Police	AO		Chief	BoV		MO		Govr		EdO	Chap	AG	Offr		Hm	PWO
1.3	1.4		2.2	2.4		2.8		3.6		3.8	3.8	3.9	3.9		4.4	4.4

Key: Govr – Governor; Hm – Housemaster; AG – AG in prison; Chief – Chief Officer; Offr – Basic grade officer; MO – Medical officer; Chap – Chaplain; PWO – Prison Welfare Officer; EdO – Education Officer; AO – Administration Officer; BoV – Member of Board of Visitors; Police – Police Officer.

Figure 2.2: Means and Studentized Clusters for Elements on the Construct 'Discipline'

Occasion I –

MO	Chap	PWO	AO	EdO
1.4	1.5	1.6	1.8	1.8

BoV	Police
2.6	3.0

AG	Hm	Govr	Offr	Chief
4.3	4.4	4.4	4.6	4.7

Occasion II –

Chap	AO	PWO	EdO	MO
1.5	1.6	1.6	1.8	1.9

Police	BoV
3.2	3.3

Hm	AG	Govr	Chief	offr
4.1	4.2	4.6	4.8	4.9

Occasion III –

AO	PWO	Chap	EdO	MO
1.6	1.6	1.6	1.7	1.8

Police	BoV
3.3	3.6

Hm	AG	Govr	Offr	Chief
3.9	4.3	4.6	4.8	5.0

Key: Govr – Governor; Hm – Housemaster; AG – AG in prison; Chief – Chief Officer; Offr – Basic grade Officer; MO – Medical Officer; Chap – Chaplain; PWO – Prison Welfare Officer; EdO – Education Officer; AO – Administration Officer; BoV – Member of Board of Visitors; Police – Police Officers.

'Care about inmates' reveals something of the same pattern (Figure 2.3) where all the specialists are distinctively associated with this construct, in contrast to uniformed staff, at least initially. Here, too, the officer is detached from the chief officer and comes to be associated a little more closely with this construct as time proceeds.

What is, perhaps, already evident from these three constructs is that although they differentiate uniformed and specialist staff, they do not differentiate governor grades, who are invariably found amongst those most closely associated with each construct. This confirms the pattern revealed by the principal component analysis, namely that all constructs tend to cluster around the governor grades. This suggests that governor grades are not associated exclusively with any particular function, but have a generic concern for the establishment as a whole.

This interpretation is consistent with the pattern revealed on the construct 'managers' which also shows a considerable stability throughout the period (Figure 2.4). Here the governor grades are seen as having near-exclusive concern for management, especially at first. However, the meaning of 'managers' would not appear to refer to a distinctive specialist contribution or skill, but to a position of central authority and involvement with all the functions of the establishment, rather than a partial concern with some exclusive function.

In this respect, then, it does seem that recruits satisfy one of the characteristics of identification, namely that the future role tends to dominate the perception of all others. The governor grades seem, to recruits, to be involved in everything that matters, compared to which others have impoverished partial functions. In other respects, too, recruits generally identify with their future role. They evaluate the governor grades quite highly, both in their own eyes and in the eyes of others. This is, perhaps, less surprising than the attenuation that this receives during the period of their socialization.

Governor grades were those most closely associated with the construct 'do the real job in the prison' (Figure 2.5), if not exclusively so, on the first occasion the test was administered. However, the officer's role comes to assume a position of pre-eminence on this construct by the final test, which is consistent with the increased association of that role with the constructs 'rehabilitate

Figure 2.3: Means and Studentized Clusters for Elements on the Construct 'Care About Inmates'

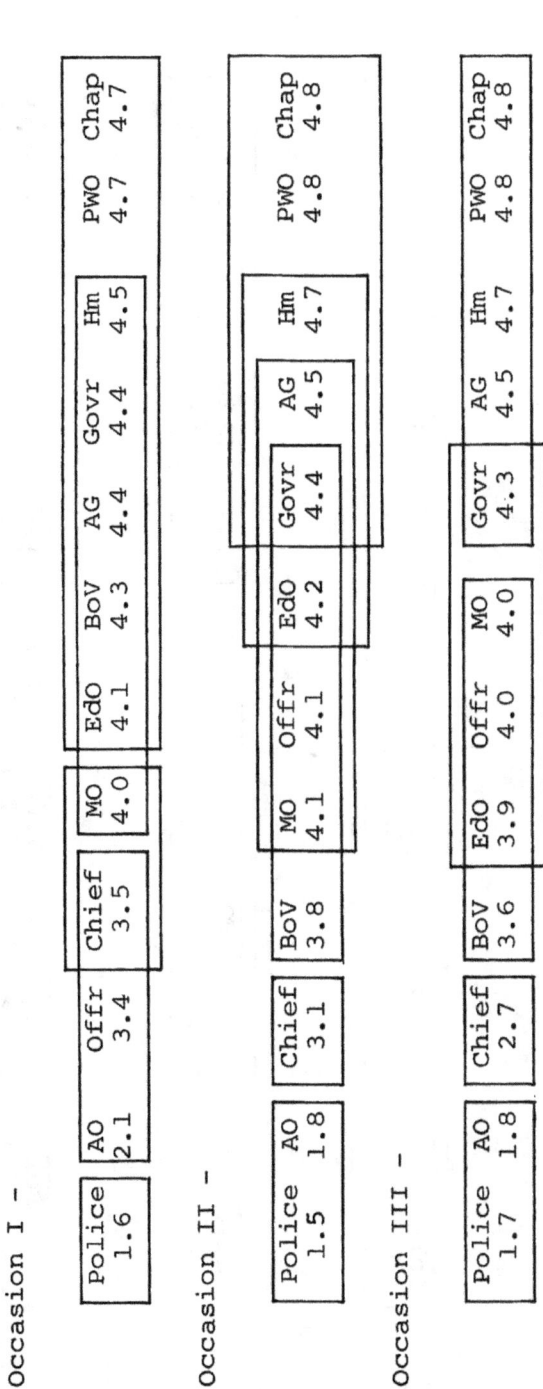

Occasion I –

Police	AO	Offr	Chief	MO	EdO	BoV	AG	Govr	Hm	PWO	Chap
1.6	2.1	3.4	3.5	4.0	4.1	4.3	4.4	4.4	4.5	4.7	4.7

Occasion II –

Police	AO	Chief	BoV	MO	Offr	EdO	Govr	AG	Hm	PWO	Chap
1.5	1.8	3.1	3.8	4.1	4.1	4.2	4.4	4.5	4.7	4.8	4.8

Occasion III –

Police	AO	Chief	BoV	EdO	Offr	MO	Govr	AG	Hm	PWO	Chap
1.7	1.8	2.7	3.6	3.9	4.0	4.0	4.3	4.5	4.7	4.8	4.8

Key: Govr – Governor; Hm – Housemaster; AG – AG in prison; Chief – Chief Officer; Offr – Basic grade Officer; MO – Medical Officer; Chap – Chaplain; PWO – Prison Welfare Officer; EdO – Education Officer; AO – Administration Officer; BoV – Member of Board of Visitors; Police – Police Officer.

51

Figure 2.4: Means and Studentized Clusters for Elements on the Construct 'Managers'

Occasion I –

Police	BoV	Chap	Offr	MO	PWO	EdO	AO	Chief	Hm	AG	Govr
1.5	1.6	1.9	2.2	2.3	2.3	2.8	3.4	4.0	4.6	4.6	4.9

Occasion II –

Police	BoV	Chap	PWO	Offr	MO	EdO	AO	Chief	Hm	AG	Govr
1.5	1.7	2.1	2.1	2.2	2.6	3.4	4.2	4.5	4.6	4.7	4.9

Occasion III –

BoV	Police	Chap	PWO	Offr	MO	EdO	AO	Hm	Chief	AG	Govr
1.8	1.8	1.9	2.0	2.2	2.8	3.4	4.3	4.4	4.5	4.7	5.0

Key: Govr – Governor; Hm – Housemaster; AG – AG in prison; Chief – Chief Officer; Offr – Basic grade Officer; MO – Medical Officer; Chap – Chaplain; PWO – Prison Welfare Officer; EdO – Education Officer; AO – Administration Officer; BoV – Member of Board of Visitors; Police – Police Officer.

Figure 2.5: Means and Studentized Clusters for Elements on the Construct 'Do the REAL Job in Prison'

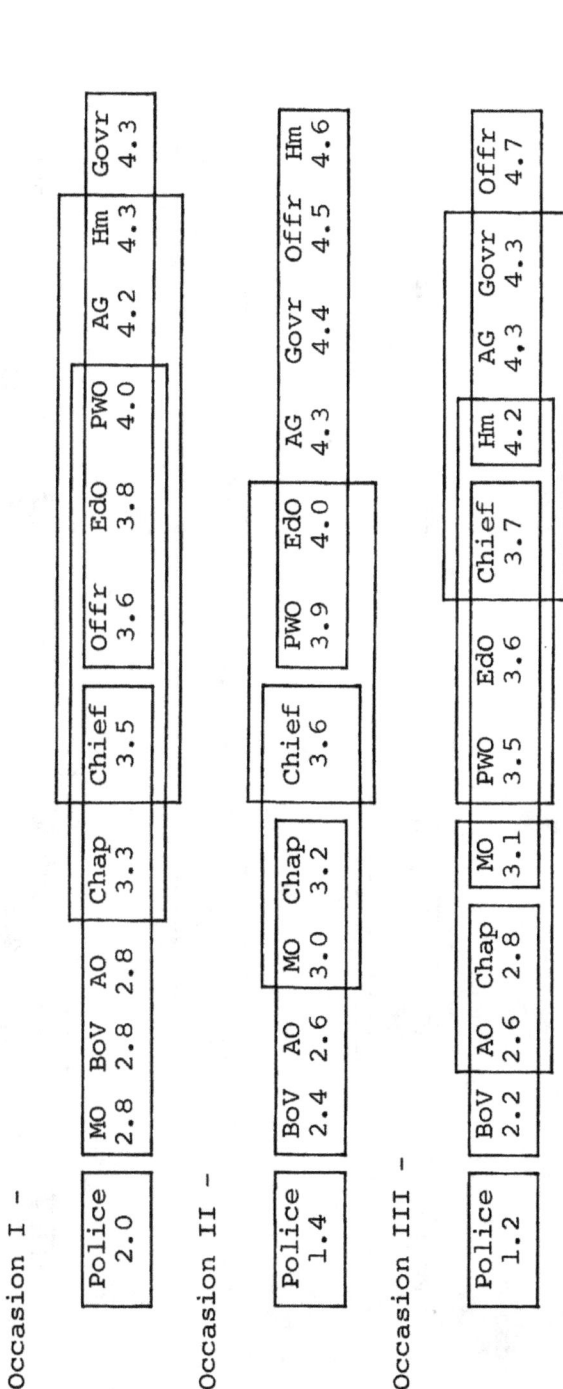

Occasion I –

Police	MO	BoV	AO	Chap	Chief	Offr	EdO	PWO	AG	Hm	Govr
2.0	2.8	2.8	2.8	3.3	3.5	3.6	3.8	4.0	4.2	4.3	4.3

Occasion II –

Police	BoV	AO	MO	Chap	Chief	PWO	EdO	AG	Govr	Offr	Hm
1.4	2.4	2.6	3.0	3.2	3.6	3.9	4.0	4.3	4.4	4.5	4.6

Occasion III –

Police	BoV	AO	Chap	MO	PWO	EdO	Chief	Hm	AG	Govr	Offr
1.2	2.2	2.6	2.8	3.1	3.5	3.6	3.7	4.2	4.3	4.3	4.7

Key: Govr – Governor; Hm – Housemaster; AG – AG in prison; Chief – Chief Officer; Offr – Basic grade officer; MO – Medical officer; Chap – Chaplain; PWO – Prison Welfare Officer; EdO – Education Officer; AO – Administration officer; BoV – Member of Board of Visitors; Police – Police Officer.

Figure 2.6: Means and Studentized Clusters for Elements on the Construct 'Have High Standing in the Prison'

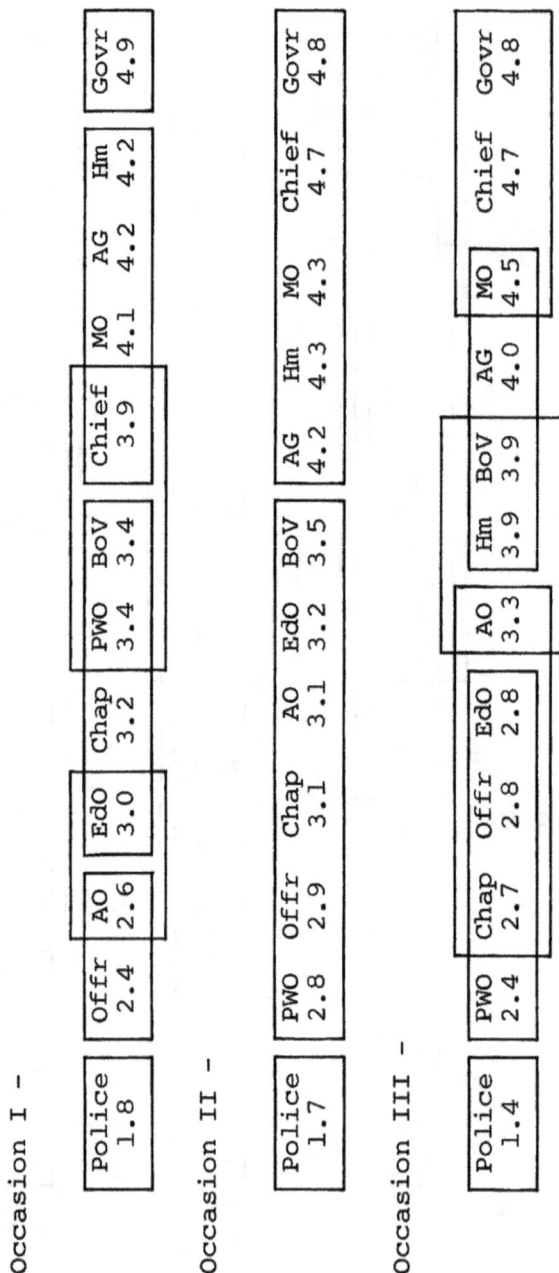

Occasion I –

| Police 1.8 | Offr 2.4 | AO 2.6 | EdO 3.0 | Chap 3.2 | PWO 3.4 | BoV 3.4 | Chief 3.9 | MO 4.1 | AG 4.2 | Hm 4.2 | Govr 4.9 |

Occasion II –

| Police 1.7 | PWO 2.8 | Offr 2.9 | Chap 3.1 | AO 3.1 | EdO 3.2 | BoV 3.5 | AG 4.2 | Hm 4.3 | MO 4.3 | Chief 4.7 | Govr 4.8 |

Occasion III –

| Police 1.4 | PWO 2.4 | Chap 2.7 | Offr 2.8 | EdO 2.8 | AO 3.3 | Hm 3.9 | BoV 3.9 | AG 4.0 | MO 4.5 | Chief 4.7 | Govr 4.8 |

Key: Govr – Governor; Hm – Housemaster; AG – AG in prison; Chief – Chief Officer; Offr – Basic grade Officer; MO – Medical Officer; Chap – Chaplain; PWO – Prison Welfare Officer; EdO – Education Officer; AO – Administration Officer; BoV – Member of Board of Visitors; Police – Police Officer.

Figure 2.7: Means and Studentized Clusters for Elements on the Construct 'Like I'd Like To Be'

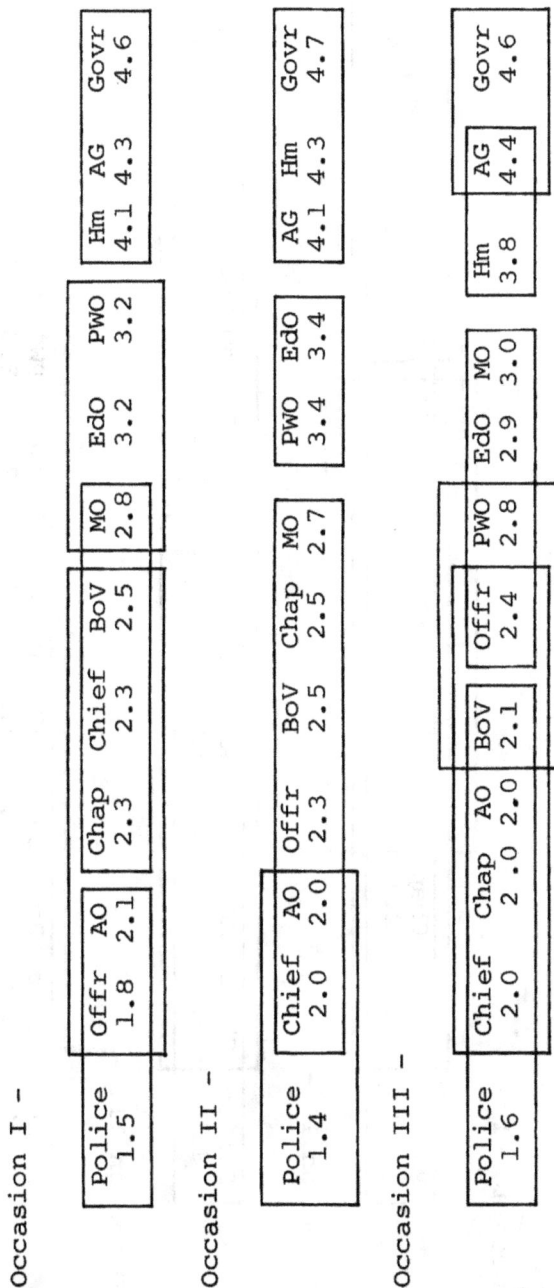

Occasion I –

| Police 1.5 | Offr 1.8 | AO 2.1 | Chap 2.3 | Chief 2.3 | BoV 2.5 | MO 2.8 | EdO 3.2 | PWO 3.2 | Hm 4.1 | AG 4.3 | Govr 4.6 |

Occasion II –

| Police 1.4 | Chief 2.0 | AO 2.0 | Offr 2.3 | BoV 2.5 | Chap 2.5 | MO 2.7 | PWO 3.4 | EdO 3.4 | AG 4.1 | Hm 4.3 | Govr 4.7 |

Occasion III –

| Police 1.6 | Chief 2.0 | Chap 2.0 | AO 2.0 | BoV 2.1 | Offr 2.4 | PWO 2.8 | EdO 2.9 | MO 3.0 | Hm 3.8 | AG 4.4 | Govr 4.6 |

Key: Govr – Governor; Hm – Housemaster; AG – AG in prison; Chief – Chief Officer; Offr – Basic grade Officer; MO – Medical Officer; Chap – Chaplain; PWO – Prison Welfare Officer; EdO – Education Officer; AO – Administration Officer; BoV – Member of Board of Visitors; Police – Police Officer.

Figure 2.8: Means and Studentized Clusters for Elements on the Construct 'Like I Am'

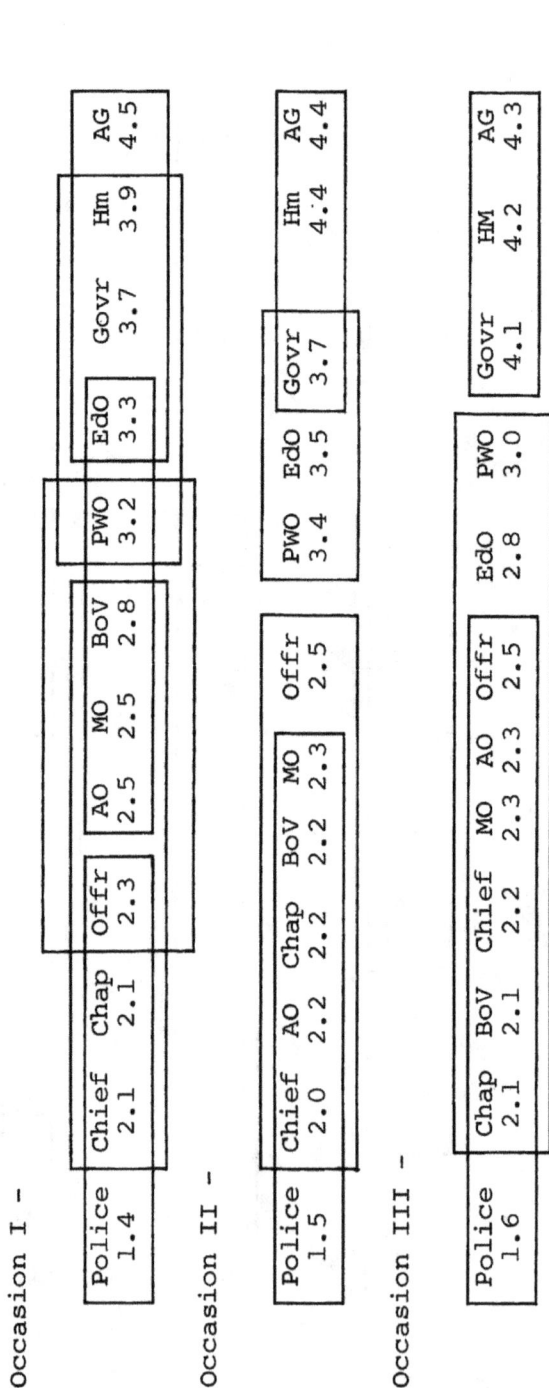

Occasion I –

Police	Chief	Chap	Offr	AO	MO	BoV	PwO	EdO	Govr	Hm	AG
1.4	2.1	2.1	2.3	2.5	2.5	2.8	3.2	3.3	3.7	3.9	4.5

Occasion II –

Police	Chief	AO	Chap	BoV	MO	Offr	PwO	EdO	Govr	Hm	AG
1.5	2.0	2.2	2.2	2.2	2.3	2.5	3.4	3.5	3.7	4.4	4.4

Occasion III –

Police	Chap	BoV	Chief	MO	AO	Offr	EdO	PwO	Govr	HM	AG
1.6	2.1	2.1	2.2	2.3	2.3	2.5	2.8	3.0	4.1	4.2	4.3

Key: Govr – Governor; Hm – Housemaster; AG – AG in prison; Chief – Chief Officer; Offr – Basic grade Officer; MO – Medical Officer; Chap – Chaplain; PWO – Prison Welfare Officer; EdO – Education Officer; AO – Administration Officer; BoV – Board of Visitors; Police – Police Officer.

inmates' and 'care about inmates'. Nevertheless,
the governor grades are displaced only by this role,
whereas on the construct 'have high standing in the
prison' (Figure 2.6) the two assistant governor
grades are displaced by the chief officer, the
medical officer and, in one instance, the member of
the board of visitors.

Nevertheless, recruits maintain a constant
desire to become like all members of the governor
grades, to judge, at least, from their responses to
the construct 'Like I would like to be' (Figure 2.7).
This, too, is consistent with the general characteristics of identification, as is the tendency to
define themselves as belonging to the role. The
construct 'Like I am now' (Figure 2.8) shows that
they identified themselves as members of the
governor grades throughout, but did so more exclusively as socialization proceeded.

Just as significant perhaps as any of the
features described so far, is the position of the
police officer role, who on every construct except
'discipline', is almost invariably placed in the
lowest position and is frequently distinguished from
all other elements. This looks suspiciously as
though this element is what grid analysts call
'massgebend':

> If one salient element is sharply distinguished
> from the rest the contrast between it and them
> may well form the most important axis or
> standard according to which the rest are judged,
> and for this reason the German word massgebend,
> perhaps best translated as trend-setting, has
> been used to describe it.[8]

There are three ways the principal components analysis can indicate whether an element is massgebend
or not. The first is the sums of squares for
elements, which if high indicates that the element
is consistently rated either positively or negatively, as opposed to respondents being indifferent
to it. Secondly, there is the total variation about
construct means, which, if large, indicates a simple
construct system, with all constructs giving
convergent results, that is being repeatedly rated
in a similar way. Thirdly, there is the percentage
of the total variation accounted for by the various
elements, when, again, if a given element has a
large percentage it indicates that it is much more
important than the others. On all three of these
indices, the police officer emerges as 'massgebend'.[9]

The significance of the police officer being
'massgebend' lies in its relationship to the simpli-

city of the grids, for three-quarters of the
recruits had grids in which two principal components
accounted for more than 60 per cent of the total
variance. The main dimension of these simple grids
would appear to be a differentiation between the
police as an out-group and those within the prison
system as an in-group. Governor grades, therefore,
emerge as the most inside of the insiders, being the
polar opposites of the police officer.

In other words, recruits drew a simple distinction between those involved in prison work and those
not, seeing the governor as the most involved,
apparently because of his multi-functional role.
This was the simple distinction that remained
unchangingly at the heart of recruits' perceptions
of the organization they were about to enter. It
was one which displayed a high, though little
changing, identification with their future role.
Its very obviousness, however, suggests that
recruits constructions were crude and remained so
throughout their socialization, showing no signs of
the increased perceptual sophistication they might
have been expected to develop.

Interviews
Little change was also found in recruits' replies to
interview questions addressed to identification.
Thus, when recruits were asked to rank order ten
occupations, not connected with the prison system,
from those most similar to those least similar to
the AG, there was little change.[10] Initially, the
headmaster was seen as having most in common with
AGs, with the personnel manager closely behind and
then the social worker. By the final interview, the
first two had exchanged positions and the social
worker had fallen a little further behind, whilst
retaining its rank order. The lorry driver and
salesman continued to be seen as the occupations
most different from the AG.

The dissimilarity of the lorry driver and
salesman from white collar, middle class occupations,
suggests some status element in recruits' perceptions, and it was clear that the majority saw themselves as middle class. Six recruits defined
themselves continuously as 'working class', compared
to 18 who saw themselves, unchangingly as 'middle
class', with just three changing from 'working' to
'middle class' and only one in the opposite direction. This is hardly surprising in an occupation
for which a university degree or equivalent is the

normal entrance requirements.

Discussion
Thus, it appears that identification with their
future role was characteristic of recruits, albeit
based upon a rather unsophisticated perception of
the organization they were about to enter. Although
there was some suggestion of an increasing identification of themselves with the occupation, this did
not seem to rely upon their recognition of more
characteristics associated with the role, so much as
the approaching time when they would actually find
themselves in that role. Thus, although socialization succeeded in maintaining recruits' identification, the continued simplicity of their constructions suggests that it did little to strengthen it.

IDEALISM

Just as 'identification' is an ill-defined, though
important concept in socialization theory, so, too,
is 'idealism'. Only Brim defines the term at all
clearly, saying that it refers to a person perceiving actual behaviour as governed by the highest
normative standards of conduct.[11] It is to this
perceived correspondence between values and actual
practice held by those of an idealistic persuasion
that most writers implicitly refer when using the
term.
     If there is, at least, tacit agreement about
the meaning of the term, there is less agreement
about the postulated pattern of change _vis_ _a_ _vis_
idealism during the socialization process. Brim,
for example, argues that individuals are first
socialized to be idealistic, so as to entrench a
commitment to social values, and only when this has
been achieved can they be allowed to see that values
may need to be compromised in actuality.[12] On the
other hand, some have argued that in some occupations it is necessary to socialize recruits into a
'cynical' attitude. Thus, nurses, it is argued,[13]
acquire a cynical shell of self-protection, which
enables them to routinely confront suffering and
death without succumbing to emotional stress.
     Perhaps the most popular formulation is a
mixture of both these views. Lortie observed[14] that
law graduates emerged from law school believing that
legal practice was actually conducted according to
the high jurisprudential principles that they had

been taught during their course. They then suffered
a period of painful readjustment, 'reality shock',
as they came to recognise that it was not and
adopted appropriately realistic orientations instead.
Apart from the emphasis on 'shock' this view does
not differ markedly from Brim's formulation, but in
some occupations which do not isolate their recruits
from reality during formal instruction there may be
a difficult interaction between principle and
practice. Again, taking nurses as an example, they
may have classroom-based courses co-existing with
practical work on the ward, and this can produce
tension between the two.[15]

The socialization of AGs approximated most
closely to this last situation, for on the one hand
recruits faced the formal penal ideology of rehabilitation during their training in the Staff College,
whilst, on the other, they confronted the grim
realities of over-crowded Victorian prisons
virtually at the outset of their training.

Therefore, did recruits become idealistically
committed to the rehabilitative ethic, or cynically
dismissive of it as an unrealizable goal, or did
they show signs of 'reality shock'?

Repertory Grid Analysis
Since recruits were supposedly being trained to work
as AGs, it is appropriate to investigate how their
views of their future work changed during their
training. For these purposes, a repertory grid was
constructed from elements representing the typical
tasks that AGs on the pilot study reported they
did.[16] In addition, some tasks were included, not
because AGs did them, but because they felt strongly
that they should. One such element was 'arranging
the deployment of staff', which in most establishments is undertaken by the chief officer, but has
been a matter of contention amongst AGs for some
time.[17]

'Holding a casework interview with an inmate'
was also not something that was very common from the
pilot interviews, but again was a task which had been
traditionally associated with the borstal housemaster's role and was still given some attention in
the training course. Similarly, although few AGs
mentioned 'showing visitors to the establishment
around', when they did, they expressed themselves
most forcefully that this was an inappropriate duty
for them to perform.

The remaining elements represented, fairly

accurately, the range of duties that AGs performed
in various types of establishment. Thus, 'checking
record documents and dossiers' is a routine task in
virtually all establishments, especially local
prisons where dates of release need to be
calculated.[18] Again, AGs seemed to spend considerable time 'writing reports on inmates' progress',
'hearing inmates' formal requests to do or have
something', 'arranging wing or house activities' and
'attending policy making meetings', even if this
usually amounted to little more than the daily
morning meeting in the governor's office in which
various tasks would be allocated. Less frequently,
and chiefly in borstals, AGs would be 'chairing
meetings to decide on inmates' training and treatment'. Also infrequent were 'hearing and adjudicating on offences committed by inmates' and
'investigating an incident in the house or wing'
which would, depending on the seriousness of the
event, normally only be undertaken when the AG was
temporarily deputizing for a superior in a more
senior position.

Some of the less formal aspects of the AGs job
were also included, such as 'discussing an inmate's
progress with his relatives', or 'informally talking
over the day's events with staff', or 'informally
discussing the inmate's problems with him', or
'discussing an inmate with the prison welfare
officer', which all AGs seemed to spend quite some
time doing during the course of a normal day.

Again, in addition to the constructs elicited
from recruits through the triadic sort procedure,
each recruit was given a common set of supplied
constructs in terms of which these elements were to
be rated. Three of these were designed to refer to
the ways in which the work of the AG seems to have
been defined, that is, as either 'administrative',
or 'care about inmates' (referring to the inmate-
centred, welfare aspects of the role), or 'exercise
authority' (referring to the disciplinary element).
The remaining two constructs were 'doing the <u>real</u>
job' and 'what AGs spend most time doing' about
which more will be said shortly.

Each of the recruits' three grids was analysed
into its principal components and visually inspected.
However, in contrast to the previous grids, no
pattern at all could be discerned here. For the
first set of grids, obtained shortly after recruits
had been selected, this could be expected, since
even ex-officers might have known little about the
detailed work of the AG, although it is a little

surprising that a group selected to do the same job
should have had no common view at all about the
tasks representing that job. What is clearly much
more surprising, is that they still expressed no
common perception when they were within days of
actually beginning to do the work referred to in the
grid.

The failure to discern any pattern could, of
course, simply have been due to a lack of insight on
the part of the researcher when inspecting the grids,
but statistical tests failed to find any relationship between constructs, elements, and constructs
and elements, lurking beneath the surface. Therefore, it was decided to concentrate attention upon
the two supplied constructs which were most directly
addressed to the issue of idealism, namely 'doing
the real job' and 'what AGs spend their time doing',
referred to hereafter as the 'focal constructs'.

Some authors have argued that those in occupations have some notion of the 'core' of their job,[19]
tasks which form the raison detre of their work,
however infrequently they may be undertaken. On the
other hand, members of occupations are also thought
to be aware of the discrepancy between the 'core' of
their work and the annoyingly 'inessential' tasks
they are called upon to perform. It was in order to
identify this discrepancy that recruits were asked
to rate work tasks in terms of two focal constructs.
If they were idealistic, we might expect that they
would perceive AGs spending much of their time doing
those things that constituted, in their eyes, 'the
real job'. Whereas, if they were realistic, or
cynical, we might expect some discrepancy between
the two. What actually emerged served only to
reinforce the initial conclusion that there was no
discernible pattern of change. Despite the complexities of the data, the overall conclusion is clear,
that recruits' individual views were highly diverse
and volatile, changing in ways that cancelled each
other out.

From the average ratings of each of the
elements on the two focal constructs, it would seem
that in general recruits had a much more consistent
perception of how they would actually spend their
time than of what they believed the essential core
of the job should be.[20] Writing reports on inmates
and attendance at policy-making meetings were
consistently rated as the most time consuming,
whereas they expected little time would be taken up
in discussing inmates with their relatives,
escorting visitors around and deploying staff.

Between these two extremes there was some adjustment
during the period. The hearing of inmates' formal
requests showed the most marked change: from moderately time-consuming on the first occasion to much
more so on the last. Holding casework interviews
and liaising with the welfare officer both showed a
gradual change in the opposite direction. Recruits
were much less consistent in their assessment of how
much time would be devoted to discussing informally
an inmate's problems, or adjudicating on offences
committed by inmates, or informally talking to staff.

If recruits' perceptions of how AGs spent
their working day appears complex, their views of
what constituted the AG's 'real job' was even more
so. Again, they were clear about the extremes, that
attending policy-making meetings was 'doing the <u>real</u>
job' and deploying staff, talking to inmates'
relatives, checking records and showing visitors
around, were not. This, of course, shows some
similarity with their perceptions of how time would
be spent, as do some of the changes in the mid-range.
Those elements which came over time to be seen as
relatively essential were: hearing inmates' formal
requests, investigating incidents and adjudicating
on offences. Those which came to be regarded as
less essential were: holding casework interviews,
liaising with the welfare officer and discussing an
inmate's problems with him. Other elements showing
an inconsistent pattern of change were: the writing
of reports, chairing meetings and talking informally
to staff.

However, despite these changes, the two focal
constructs maintained a moderately high correlation
throughout the period, with Pearson correlation
coefficients of .45, .34 and .44 respectively.
However, this is misleading if it is taken to mean
that individual recruits consistently saw a
moderate degree of correlation between these two
constructs, since the mean correlation for
individuals was a startling .001, which amounts to
no correlation whatsoever. In other words,
individuals changed their minds about the degree to
which they expected these two constructs to coincide
from one occasion to the next in ways which, when
taken together, tended to cancel each other out.[21]

Much the same picture emerges from the analysis
of the other supplied constructs. Thus, 'care about
inmates', 'administration' and 'exercise authority'
provide relatively fixed points with respect to each
other throughout the period, with 'administration'
and 'exercise authority' being positively related to

each other and negatively related to 'care about inmates'.[22] When these three constructs' relation-ships to the two focal constructs is examined, it seems that there is a reasonably stable pattern.[23] Recruits show a distinct and growing bias towards seeing 'care about inmates' as having the closest connection with 'doing the real job', with 'exercise authority' and 'administration' having little association with it. However, they do not see themselves spending more time in tasks associated with 'care about inmates' than in 'administration', and over the period of their training appear to increasingly see their job as a more or less equal balance of all three aspects of the job.

Again, the apparent stability of these relationships obscures the considerable amount of individual variation beneath the surface. For example, although recruits appeared to maintain a balance between all three aspects when considering how they would spend their time, individuals tended to emphasize either devoting themselves to the care of inmates or to administration and exercising authority, but in such a way that overall these differences of emphasis cancelled themselves out.[24] Likewise, although there was a distinct bias towards seeing 'care about inmates' as more essential than the time devoted to it would warrant, this did not mean that individuals saw an exclusive commitment to caring about inmates at the expense of administ-ration and exercising authority, for on the first occasion there was a positive correlation between all three. It was only later that recruits came to see caring about inmates as being opposed to admin-istration and exercising authority. Furthermore, individuals also changed their minds considerably over time. Thus, in relation to how they envisaged spending their time, the mean correlation coefficient for 'administration' was .13, for 'exercise authority', .25, and for 'care about inmates', .18. Indeed, there was virtually no correlation between successive administrations of the construct 'administrative'. The picture is only a little more stable in the relation of these constructs to 'doing the real job' which produced mean correlations of .43 for 'administrative', .30 for 'exercise authority' and .16 for 'care about inmates'.

In sum, the apparent stability and balance in recruits' views, is belied by the actual diversity and volatility of individuals' views, which were self-cancelling when considered as a group. There-

fore, from this data, we cannot say that recruits
were idealistic or not, for some were and others
were not. What we can say is that there was <u>no</u>
pattern of change in aggregate attitudes either
towards idealism or away from it.

Why was this? Was it because the repertory
grid technique is ill-suited to the task of detec-
ting these attitudes? It does not seem so, since
the construct 'doing the <u>real</u> job' did closely
correlate with recruits' own elicited constructs
which referred to evaluations of tasks or their
essential quality.[25] However, what was also
evident, was that recruits only rarely provided such
constructs. Only two per cent of all the constructs
elicited were of this kind. In other words, it
would seem that recruits found the contrast between
the essential and inessential aspects of their work
quite meaningless. This is consistent with the
observation made above, that even at the aggregate
level, recruits were much less consistent in their
ratings of tasks in terms of 'doing the <u>real</u> job'.
It might be anticipated that recruits would change
their assessment of how they might spend their time
as AGs, as they came to discover more about the job,
but this was relatively stable. Thus, it seems
that recruits entered the occupation with little
common notion of what constituted the core of the
AG's work and acquired no such notion during
the course of their socialization. As such this
conclusion stands in complete opposition to the
majority of theoretical statements and empirical
observations on the subject.

Interviews
Like other white collar, managerial or professional
occupations, those recruited into the Prison Service
as AGs had a primarily intrinsic orientation to work,
that is, they mainly sought satisfactions from the
work itself rather than from benefits, such as pay,
which accrue from it. When asked what they felt was
important in any job, none of them referred
exclusively to extrinsic rewards and only three of
the 33 gave these rewards priority over intrinsic
benefits. For the remainder, it was the intrinsic
rewards which were the main source of satisfaction
expected from any job. This orientation to work
remained constant, but their detailed expectations
about what would prove satisfying and dissatisfying
in the AG's job revealed changes which suggest a
distinct reduction in their initial idealism.

Job Satisfaction and Idealism

When the recruits were asked what they anticipated
would be the satisfactions and dissatisfactions in
the AG's job, their replies could be classified
along five dimensions: rehabilitating inmates;
autonomy of action; amicability of working relationships with staff and inmates; personal ability to do
the job; and the knowledge that one's work was
valued by public opinion. Dissatisfactions were the
converse of each of these.

Treating each reply as a separate unit, what
can be seen immediately from Figure 2.9 is the
quite considerable decrease in recruits' reference
to rehabilitation as a criterion of job satisfaction.
At the beginning of the socialization period it was
the most commonly referred to criterion, but by the
end it had fallen to near the bottom of the list.
It was not simply that recruits began to see rehabilitation as a source of dissatisfaction arising
from high levels of reconviction, it was that they
did not mention this criterion at all. Even those
who referred to this criterion initially also
foresaw both satisfaction and dissatisfaction
arising from this source, and those who continued to
refer to it were, if anything, slightly more
inclined to see it as a source of potential satisfaction. Moreover, there were qualitative changes
in the way in which other criteria were referred to.
Initially, recruits related these other criteria to
'rehabilitation': for example, they hoped that they
would have sufficient autonomy to be able to introduce rehabilitative policies of their own. However,
by the end of their training, recruits desired
sources of satisfaction other than 'rehabilitation'
for their own sake: they now wanted autonomy of
action so as to be free of burdensome red tape.

In short, 'rehabilitation' came to be seen as
irrelevant to job satisfaction.

Resignation and Postings

There were other changes too which were consistent
with the abandonment of recruits' commitment to
rehabilitation. When discussing their first posting
to an establishment as an AG, recruits initially
showed a distinct preference for borstals and did so
because they were attracted by the intrinsic merits
of the regime and its association with the rehabilitative ethic. However, by the end of their training, just under half the recruits were posted to an
establishment other than the one for which they had

Figure 2.9: Recruits' Changing Criteria of Job
Satisfaction

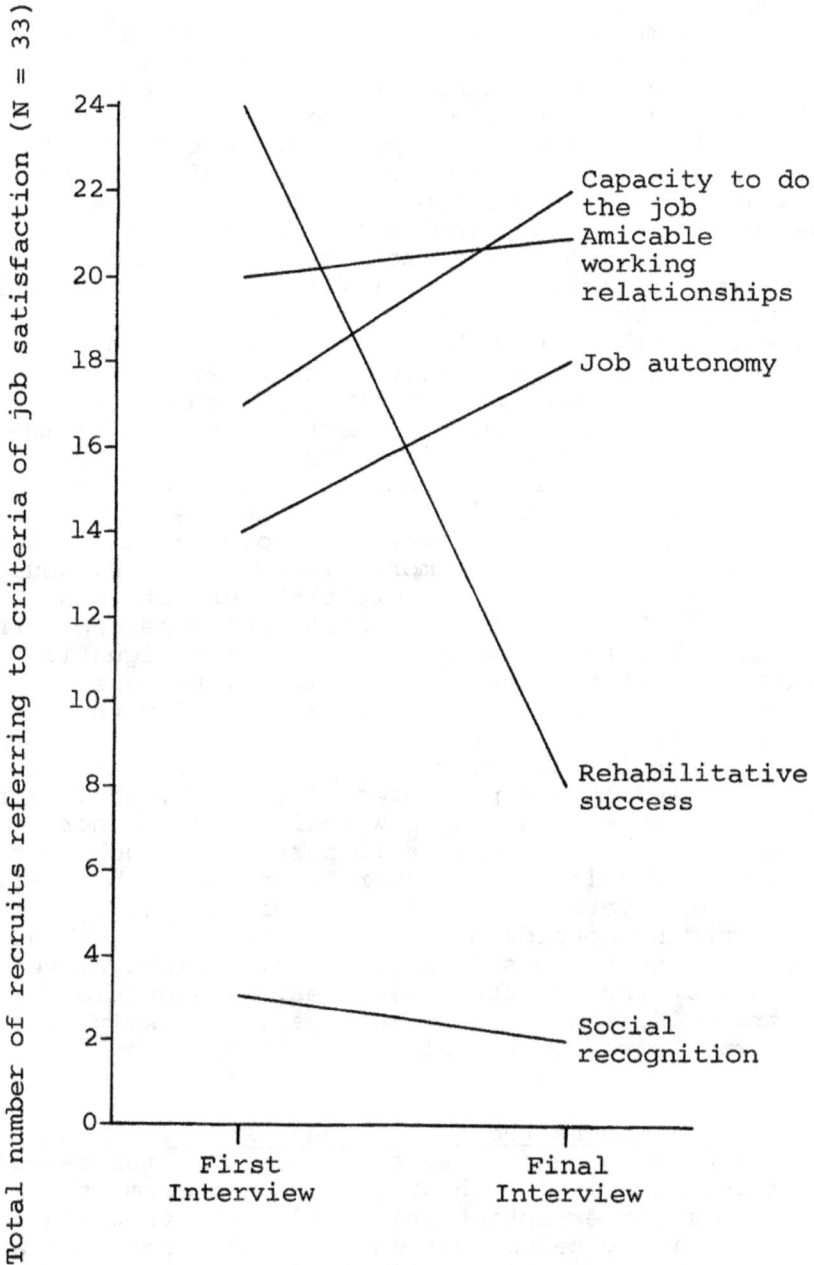

originally expressed a preference, but none of them
expressed any dissatisfaction with this.   In
describing their feelings about their postings none
mentioned the rehabilitative success, or otherwise,
of the type of establishment in which they were
going to work.

In a much broader context, too, they showed
significant disillusionment with the workings of the
criminal justice system.   Their original evaluation
of that system was relatively high, but when
measured after their initial attachment it showed a
statistically significant reduction and this low
evaluation was maintained when their attitudes were
measured during the final weeks of the course.

As their commitment to rehabilitation declined,
so their perception of their future work became less
dramatic.   This was revealed in their answers to
questions asking them how likely they thought it was
that they would ever seriously consider resigning
and what would prompt them to make such a move.
Clearly, this is a delicate matter and results must
be interpreted with caution.   Nevertheless, the
patterns of change are instructive in the context of
the foregoing discussion.   First, between the
initial and final interviews just over a third of
the recruits thought it more likely that they would
resign, whilst only one recruit thought it less
likely.[26]   Second, and more importantly perhaps, the
reasons that they gave for envisaging resignation
showed a distinct change.   Initially, the great
majority had seen resignation as something that
would be forced upon them by dramatic events outside
their control, such as being emotionally incapable
of withstanding the pressures of the job, whereas by
the final interview they saw resignation as more a
matter of voluntary choice in pursuit of such things
as improved salary.   Moreover, even those who still
saw it as a matter of compulsion, increasingly saw
more mundane considerations as compelling, such as
the frequent changes of posting which might prove
too disturbing for their families.   Resignation, in
other words, was not only seen as more likely, but
also much more conceivable.

Rehabilitation as the Aim of Penal Policy
If the picture painted so far gives the impression
that recruits lost much of initial idealism, there
was one major exception which indicates that they
did not simply become cynical, for they retained a
strong commitment to the ideal of rehabilitation as

the aim of the prison system. Whilst it was not possible to ask about these matters during the initial interview, because of constraints of time, it was possible to do so at the final interview. When asked what the Prison Service should aim to achieve, there was no doubt that most recruits gave priority to rehabilitation, with approximately half saying that it should be the exclusive aim and a further nine giving it primacy over custody. At the same time, recruits were decidedly critical of the Service's failure in this regard, with the majority saying that it either did not achieve this aim or did so only minimally. Only those few who gave priority to custody saw the Service as successfully achieving its aims.

Furthermore, when asked to say how they would like to see matters improved, recruits' proposals read like an extract from the manifesto of a liberal penal reform group. They wanted to keep all but the most dangerous offenders out of prison entirely and to have more individual training for those committed to prison within more specialized regimes. They also wanted better trained, highly paid and qualified staff, better living conditions for inmates, and an attempt to educate the public to accept more enlightened approaches to treatment. Some mentioned making offenders do more purposeful and satisfying work. On the other hand, they actually saw the Prison Service as wasteful of the resources it had, and suffering from poor physical conditions, overcrowding and poor quality of staff.

In other words, when it came to considering the Prison Service as such, rather than their own role within it, recruits still retained a commitment to rehabilitation at the end of their training, which might be taken as a measure of continuing idealism. At the same time, however, they were critically aware of the extent to which this aim was not being achieved.

Discussion
On the face of it, this evidence is largely consistent with the 'reality shock' thesis, for recruits entered the Service with something of a commitment to rehabilitation which was then all but lost during their succeeding period of socialization. The failure to find any pattern in the repertory grids dealing with the duties of AGs might also be interpreted as confirming the thesis, since recruits were not only discovering more about what the AGs

actually did, they were having their notions about what they ought to do contradicted also, their perceptions reflecting this flux.

Where the evidence diverges from the 'reality shock' thesis, is in the absence of any replacement perception of the job. AGs appear to have had their initial idealism dispelled, but not to have had some alternative conception provided by their socializing experiences. They lost their commitment to rehabilitation as a criterion of job satisfaction, but it was replaced by no other shared alternative.

In so far as the evidence is consistent with the thesis, the obvious source of 'reality shock' would be the recruits' direct experience of prison conditions, especially during the initial attachment. Were they, like entrants to other occupations that have been studied, to have entered the job with a romantically positive image of their future work, prison conditions could be expected to have destroyed it. What is surprising about AGs is that 18 of the 23 direct-entrants said they found prison conditions better than expected. They almost invariably found a surprising absence of tension, violence and oppression. As one recruit explained, it was the fact that hundreds of prisoners conformed so readily to the instructions of a handful of staff that shook him.

This amounted to a 'reality shock' because, welcome though it was to find that prisons were not bastions of brutal repression as some recruits had feared, it also meant that the scope any individual recruit would have for making positive changes was limited. If prisons were staffed by punitive authoritarians, then there may have been some scope for introducing improvements and effecting some rehabilitation, through the AG's personal commitment to humane and liberal policies. If, on the other hand, one finds that prisons are staffed largely by reasonable men and that prisoners are not repeatedly coerced into compliance, but conform more or less willingly to the regime, then there is much less that one can do to promote improvements. Since it appeared to be the system which was responsible for high rates of reconviction, to maintain 'rehabilitation' as a criterion of job satisfaction would have been irrational, since there was little the individual could do to rehabilitate inmates. However, if it is the system, rather than the people working in it, that is responsible for the failure to rehabilitate, then it makes sense to continue to believe that changes could and should be made with a view to improving it.

The 'reality shock' thesis not only applied to direct-entrants, but equally to ex-officers, who despite their experience of penal conditions were just as inclined to define job satisfaction in terms of rehabilitation. It was the policy of the Staff College to send ex-officers to a type of establishment different from that with which they were familiar. For the borstal officer this produced the same kind of 'reality shock' as confronted direct-entrants, for he was as likely to find prisons as surprisingly free from tensions as they did. Those who had previously served in prisons, on the other hand, were surprised and disillusioned to find that borstals were so similar to prisons, for many had harboured the belief that borstals were where the rehabilitation did take place, where inmates were still young enough to be receptive to influence. It was only this small group of ex-prison officers who suffered the standard form of 'reality shock' as described in the literature.

If the socialization of AGs was effective in dispelling naivete, it was decidedly ineffective in substituting a common occupational culture. Indeed, what it appeared to do was substitute dissensus for consensus: recruits were more heterogeneous in their attitudes when they completed their training than they had been before.

DIFFERENTIAL SOCIALIZATION?

The repertory grid analysis of the AG's perception of their work revealed a very high degree of variation between recruits and instability in their attitudes over time. However, variation and instability was not restricted to this analysis alone. The predominant patterns were explained above but there have frequently been exceptions, such as the quarter of recruits who did not initially mention rehabilitation in the context of job satisfactions and the other quarter who continued to do so at the end of their training.

On the face of it, this observed variation and instability is damaging to socialization theory, since it contradicts the central prediction of increasing homogeneity. It seems particularly damaging, of course, when self-cancelling change occurs, which testifies to the absence of any 'structural effect' whatsoever. Yet, in a perverse way, this evidence can be used to bolster socialization theory, since it may be taken to imply that there were, not one, but several, socialization processes taking place simultaneously.[27]

There are two ways in which differential socialization may occur. First, it is possible that even within a notionally common training course there are systematic differences in the type of socialization to which recruits are exposed. Within the Staff College recruits were divided into four tutorial groups, each under the direction of a senior AG acting as tutor. These tutors may have exerted divergent influence over their respective groups. Equally, ex-officers had completed a Pre-Course Training Programme before beginning their AG training, whilst some direct-entrants had worked as temporary officers during the months preceding the start of their training, whereas other direct-entrants had never seen inside a prison or borstal before their training began. These different experiences may all have made their divergent impact.

Second, socialization theorists have emphasized that, at least, in the case of secondary socialization, it is necessary to bear in mind the previous socializing experiences that recruits have had and which may result in differing patterns of response to current influences.[28] Clearly, there is, in the case of AG socialization, the differences in background between ex-officers and direct-entrants, and the Staff College is rich in folklore about the different ways in which these two groups respond to training. Ex-officers were thought to be more authoritarian, punitive and generally conservative in their attitudes towards crime and punishment, and less caring towards inmates. Their lack of educational qualifications was also supposed to leave them anxious about the training course's academic content, which manifested itself in a tendency to reject such content out-of-hand. On the other hand, direct-entrants were thought by staff of the Staff College to be more radical, liberal and humane in their attitudes, but more anxious about working within a prison context. They, too, were thought to react negatively to the academic content of the training course, but in their case because in making it intelligible to ex-officers, lecturers were unable to stimulate direct-entrants already familiar with the material.

There were other distinctions which might also have been drawn between recruits, such as that between the younger graduates for whom this was their first job and their relatively older colleagues. There were those who were defined by others and who defined themselves as 'radicals' or 'idealists', and who might have reacted differently to their less 'radical' and less 'idealistic' colleagues to their common socialization. Social-izing agents may also have treated those who were destined for a prison posting differently from those who were to be posted to borstals.

However, the application of these distinctions did little to explain the variation and instability of recruits' attitudes, and what differences they did make were largely marginal and ad hoc. The findings are explained in detail below to demonst-rate just how marginal they are and how the theory obtains no support from the notion of differential socialization. Thus, ex-officers were found, not surprisingly, to see resignation as least likely, although they too showed the same trend towards reduced commitment between the beginning and end of their training. However, since ex-officers had become socially mobile as a result of their promo-tion and had few transferable skills or qualific-ations which would allow them to maintain their newly-found status outside the Prison Service this can hardly be counted as a major observation. On the other hand, in their evaluations of the criminal justice system, ex-officers were indistinguishable from direct-entrants who had been previously employed, but these two groups together were signif-icantly more favourable in their evaluations than graduate direct-entrants. This was a difference that was maintained throughout the period of training, although all three groups showed the same L-shaped pattern of attitude change.

There were some highly marginal differences in the patterns of identification. Thus, ex-officers saw a greater association between governor grades and the construct 'care about inmates' than did either group of direct-entrants, which is surprising in view of their supposedly less caring attitude. Also, ex-officers saw the two AG grades as less associated with the construct 'managers' than they saw the governor, whereas direct-entrants tended to group the AG in a prison together with the governor as more closely associated with this construct than the housemaster. However, the significance of this pattern is not at all clear. What is clear is that the application of this difference between ex-officers and direct-entrants contributes very little to our understanding of the various patterns of change exhibited by recruits in general.

Again, there are to be found some equally
marginal patterns of change amongst those defined as
'radical' because of their views on crime and
punishment. They were neither consistently idealistic or pessimistic about the AG's job, as estimated by the correlation between the constructs 'what
AGs spend their time doing' and 'doing the <u>real</u> job'.
What did emerge was that radicals were more volatile
in their attitudes than other recruits, showing
significantly more change between each of the three
test occasions than others. Again, although
radicals were no more likely to refer to rehabilitation as a criterion of job satisfaction, they were
more likely to have abandoned it by the end of their
training. On the other hand, whilst they were more
likely to envisage themselves resigning initially,
they were no more likely to do so at the time of the
final interview. Finally, no radical felt that the
proper aim of the prison system should be custody
and none believed that the Service was doing a good
job as they defined it. This contrasts with the
half of the remainder who did, at least, see some
role for custody as an aim of the system and the
third who felt that the Service was doing a good job.
    The differences between those posted to prisons
as opposed to borstals was not what differential
socialization would lead us to expect. It was that
those posted to borstal were either optimistic <u>or</u>
pessimistic, as measured by the correlation between
the two focal constructs, whilst those going to
prisons were moderate. This may represent the
higher hopes and forebodings of disappointment that
recruits held for borstals, as opposed to the more
mundane expectations that they attached to prisons.
    The only structural difference that could be
detected between tutorial groups was perverse indeed,
showing, if anything, the exact opposite of what
socialization theory predicts. On the first test
occasion, those who would eventually enter one
tutorial group were significantly optimistic, whilst
those who would enter another group were significantly pessimistic as measured by the correlation
between focal constructs, with the remainder in-
between. However, at this point the tutorial groups
were not in existence, recruits had met neither
their tutor nor each other, and no one knew who
would be allocated to each tutorial. Nor could
there be any suggestion that those of an identif-
iably optimistic or pessimistic persuasion were
allocated to certain groups and not others, since,
firstly, the information necessary for such an

allocation was not available, and, secondly, it was policy to maintain balance between each group on every known criterion.

Furthermore, by the second test occasion, attitudes had changed so that now the tutorial groups were no longer statistically significantly different from each other. This process of individual change continued so that by the final test occasion the tutorial groups were significantly alike, but only in the extent of their internal diversity.

The reason for detailing all the ways in which these variables permit ad hoc explanations of marginal patterns of change, is to demonstrate the lengths it is necessary to go to in order to achieve any sort of explanation at all. Enough has been said, perhaps, to show that the absence of any patterns of change in the main attitudes goes unexplained by anything described above. It would be tedious and unproductive to detail all the areas on which differences between types of recruit were sought but not found. Suffice to say that there were no discoverable differences between ex-officers, changed career and graduate direct-entrants in any of the following analyses: the correlation between the two focal constructs; the volatility or stability of this correlation between tests; the variance of these correlations; the salience of the construct 'doing the real job'; recruits' extrinsic or intrinsic orientation to work; the reference to rehabilitation as a criterion of job satisfaction; voluntary or compulsory motive for resigning; the evaluation of the Prison Service; whether or not rehabilitation should be the aim of the prison system; how to improve the system; or the total correlation between governor grades on the role grid.

Nor is this all. There was no difference between radicals and others in: their general orientation to work; their reference to rehabilitation as a criterion of job satisfaction; voluntary or compulsory reasons for resigning; initial reactions to prison reality; or proposals for improving the prison system. Similarly, those who describe themselves as 'idealistic', that is, claimed to have joined the Service out of relgious, moral, social or political motives, showed no discernibly different patterns of change compared to others. Moreover, none of the structural differences in socialization experience accounted for any of the diversity that had been observed.

Of course, the difficulty with this exercise is

that it is impossible, in principle, to prove conclusively what philosophers call a 'negative existential proposition', because however many types of recruit are identified there may be some other, as yet unrecognised, grouping that would account for the variation observed. One way to approach the problem is inductively and see if any groupings emerge on any particular variable. This is a time-consuming process, which, in any case, can only be executed on quantitative variables. Thus, one variable was selected at random and an analysis carried out. The variable in question was the degree of correlation between governor grades and the constructs 'managers', 'discipline', and 'care about inmates'. Not only were there no discernible groupings, when subjected to a studentized range analysis, the size of the groups and the pattern of overlap between them was wholly consistent with them forming a range. Thus, although the extremes were significantly different, on two of the three constructs, the most inclusive group contained two-thirds or more of the total number of recruits.

On this evidence, therefore, it would seem to be as certain as it is possible to be, that no pattern of differential socialization accounts for the variation and instability of recruits' attitudes. Certainly, there is no warrant for supposing that any of the obvious differences or those most widely emphasized by Staff College folklore account for any significant part of this variation.

SUMMARY AND CONCLUSIONS

The purpose of this chapter has been to describe what, if any, patterns of change emerged as AG recruits passed through their initial training and socialization. It was shown that recruits had a reasonably clear, albeit somewhat simple, perception of the Prison Service, in which the governor grades were seen as central, generically involved with all the functions of the establishment. This general picture changed little during the period, as did recruits' identification with the governor grades, although there was some indication that identific-ation became more exclusively directed towards governors as time passed. There was also little change in the wider aspects of identification with occupations outside the Prison Service and with social class.

What did show some considerable change was

recruits' commitment to rehabilitation as a
criterion of job satisfaction. This declined as
recruits appeared to substitute a mundane conception
of prison work for the dramatic notions with which
they had entered. They did not become disillusioned
with the rehabilitative aim as such, but came to see
it as a matter of penal policy which was out of
their hands, rather than something they could
achieve as individuals through their commitment to
humane and liberal values.

If this reflected a reduction in naive idealism,
what was surprising was that socialization provided
no substitute conception of the job. This was
particularly apparent from the fact that recruits
had no clear and agreed notion of the work they were
to do as AGs. Whilst one might have expected that
their view of the AG's role would be inchoate at the
beginning of their socialization, given their lack
of knowledge, it is very surprising indeed that only
days before they actually began working as AGs their
views were so diverse as to defy codification. Nor
could the variability and instability of their
attitudes as a whole be explained by differential
socialization, for neither the structural differences in their training nor their prior experiences
could account for more than the most marginal
variations. In sum, as a group, they identified
with a role they seemed to know little about.

Considering the evidence as a whole, it appears
that socialization theory, as it is conventionally
understood, as the transformation of culturally
heterogeneous collection of individuals into a
functionally homogeneous group, did not apply to AGs.

NOTES

1. For a discussion of the role of identific-
ation in childhood socialization, see: E.Q. Campbell,
'The Internalization of moral norms', Sociometry,
1964, vol. 27 (4), pp 391-412; R. Hartley, 'A
Developmental View of Female Sex-Role Identification'
in B.J. Biddle and E. Thomas (eds), Role Theory
(New York, Wiley, 1966); and E.E. Maccoby, 'The
Taking of Adult Roles in Middle Childhood' in
K. Danziger (ed), Readings in Child Socialization
(London, Pergamon, 1970).

For a discussion of the role of this variable
in occupational socialization, see: H.S. Becker and
J. Carper, 'Professional Identification' in H.H.
Vollmer and D. Mills (eds), Professionalization
(Englewood Cliffs, Prentice Hall, 1966); E.C. Hughes,

Men and Their Work (Glencoe, Free Press, 1958);
C. Sofer, Men in Mid-Career (Cambridge University
Press, 1970); R. Dubin, 'Industrial Workers' Worlds:
a Study in the Central Life Interests of Industrial
Workers', in A.M. Rose (ed), Human Behaviour and
Social Process (London, Routledge, 1962); L. Orzack,
'The Idea of Work as a Central Life Interest of
Professionals', Social Problems, 1959, vol 7 (1),
pp 125-32; E. Quarantelli, 'School-learned Adjust-
ment to Negative Self-images in High Status
Occupational Roles: the Dental Student Example',
Journal of Educational Sociology, 1961, vol. 35 (1),
pp 165-71; I. Simpson, 'Patterns of Socialization in
Professions: the Case of the Student Nurse',
Sociological Inquiry, 1967, vol. 37 (1), pp 47-54;
D. Berlew and D. Hall, 'The Socialization of
Managers: Effects of Expectations on Performance',
Administrative Science Quarterly, 1966, vol. 2 (2),
pp 207-23; B. Varley, 'Socialization in Social Work
Education', Social Work, 1963, July, pp 102-09.

2. The principal components describe the underlying common axes in terms of which all the data may
be arranged and these axes themselves are ordered
according to the proportion of the total variation
in the intercorrelation matrix they explain. Thus,
constructs and elements which are heavily 'loaded'
onto the most important components, may be
considered more salient for the person, since it is
in terms of these constructs that he construes his
environment as represented by the elements. For
further explanation, see P. Slater, The Measurement
of Intrapersonal Space by Grid Technique (vols 1 & 2,
London, Wiley, 1976).

3. The role titles were obtained from pilot
interviews held with serving AGs in the northern
region of the Prison Service, who were asked to
describe the work they had done the previous day and
with whom they had dealt whilst doing it, as well as
an account of their routine duties. The roles
represent the spectrum of those with whom AGs have
routine contact from the most to the least often.

4. The controversy surrounding the role of
'police officer' lay in the reaction of many AGs to
the police, both during pilot interviews and at the
Staff College. Although the police are part of the
administration of justice and are also involved in
prison security, and therefore appearing to have
close contact with the Prison Service, AGs seemed to
dislike and distrust them. On one occasion, a
senior tutor described how he had spoken to students
at a nearby police training centre and sensing the

the hostility from the police, had said 'I know what you're thinking: "We (the police) catch them and you (the Prison Service) lose them"'. In view of this strength of feeling it was decided to have the role of 'police officer' represent the wider context of the administration of justice.

5. Note: supplied constructs are administered only at the end of the elicitation procedure to avoid suggesting to respondents how the researcher construes the elements.

6. Analysis of variance does share many of the most basic parametric assumptions of principal components analysis, but avoids the necessity of 'normalizing' the raw scores and approaches the analysis of data through tests of statistical significance rather than through correlational analysis.

7. I am greately indebted to the late Mr. A.B. Royce, Senior Lecturer, Department of Sociology, University of Leeds, who introduced me to and explained the studentized range statistic.

The aim of the studentized range statistic is to compare a series of sample means in an array and determine which are significantly different from each other. In order to compensate for the fact that a series of sample means are drawn from a population of such means with the attendant sampling error, the level of statistical significance which differences between each successive pair of means must satisfy, becoming progressively more stringent. Of the three methods available, the one used was the 'Tukey C'. For further details see, B. Winer, Statistical Principles in Experimental Design (2nd edn., New York, McGraw-Hill, 1972) and L. Harter, D. Clemm and E. Guthrie, The Probability Integrals of the Range and of the Studentized Range (W.A.D.C. Technical Papers, Rep. 58-484, vol. 2, Wright Air Development Centre, 1959).

8. P. Slater, Notes on Ingrid 72 (Institute of Psychiatry, Denmark Hill, London, pp 6-7).

9. For further details see, P.A.J. Waddington, The Occupational Socialization of Prison Governor Grades (unpublished Ph.D. thesis, University of Leeds, 1977, pp 117-19)

10. The full list of occupations and their mean rankings were as follows:

Occupation:	First interview	Final interview
Headmaster	2.3	2.4
Personnel Manager	2.3	1.9
Social Worker	2.5	3.0
Army Officer	3.2	3.2
Clergyman	4.1	4.5
Bank Manager	4.4	4.0
Trade Union Official	4.6	4.5
Policeman	4.2	4.5
Salesman	5.6	5.3
Lorry Driver	6.8	6.9

11. O.G. Brim, 'Socialization Through the Life Cycle', in O.G. Brim and S. Wheeler, Socialization After Childhood: Two Essays (New York, Wiley, 1966).

12. Ibid.

13. I. Menzies, 'A Case Study in the Function of Social Systems as a Defense Against Anxiety', Human Relations, 1960, vol. 13 (1), pp 95-122.

14. D. Lortie, 'Professional Socialization' in Vollmer and Mills (eds), op cit.

15. V.L. Olesen and E.W. Whittaker, The Silent Dialogue (San Francisco, Jossey-Bass, 1968); M. Colledge, 'Professional Socialization of the Student Nurse' (unpublished paper read to the British Sociological Association Annual Conference, 'Health, Illness and Society', May, 1976)

16. These elements were obtained through the same means as for the role grid, see p 78f.

17. See pp 13,15.

18. When a prisoner is convicted the prison authorities must calculate his 'Earliest Date of Release' (E.D.R.) and Latest Date of Release (L.D.R.). These routine computations are complex because of the vagaries of the calender and intricacies of the sentencing process. They are also important, since the governor is individually responsible for releasing prisoners at the correct time.

19. See Hughes, op cit, pp 121-23.

20. For further information, see Waddington, op cit, Table 5.X, pp 152-53.

21. Ibid, Table 5.XI, p 154.

22. Ibid, Table 5.I, p 144.

23. Ibid, Table 5.VIII, p 150.

24. Ibid, Table 5.IX, p 151.

25. Ibid, Table 5.XIV, p 157.

26. Ibid, Table 4.XV, p 123.

27. For further discussion of 'differential socialization', see: O.G. Brim, 'Personality development as role-learning' in I. Iscoe and H. Stevenson (eds), <u>Personality Development in Children</u> (Austin, University of Texas, 1960); J. Alutto, L. Hrebiniak and R. Alonso, 'A Study of Differential Socialization for Members of One Professional Group', <u>Journal of Health and Social Behaviour</u>, 1971, vol. 12 (2), pp 140-47; G. Miller and L. Wager, 'Adult Socialization, Organizational Structure and Role Orientations', <u>Administrative Science Quarterly</u>, 1971, vol. 16 (2), pp 151-63; W.L. Wallace, 'Institutional and Life-Cycle Socialization of College Freshmen', <u>American Journal of Sociology</u>, 1964, vol. 120 (3), pp 303-18.

28. See: Miller and Wager, ibid; Wallace, ibid; and R.B. Warnecke, 'Non-intellectual Factors Related Attrition from a Collegiate Nursing Program', <u>Journal of Health and Social Behaviour</u>, 1973, vol. 14 (2), pp 153-65.

Chapter Three

THE ORGANIZATION AND MANAGEMENT OF TRAINING

INTRODUCTION

The question that now presents itself is why the
Prison Service Staff College had so little influence
on recruits' attitudes and certainly less than an
'assimilating institution' might be expected to have.
In seeking an answer to this question we will need
to examine both the agents and recipients of socialization to see in which ways they departed from the
model of an assimilating institution.

In this chapter we shall concentrate upon the
role of the socializing agents, principally the AGs
Course Tutors, and examine how the AGs Course was
organized and managed on a day-to-day basis.
Socialization research only rarely reports upon the
actions of socializing agents and then usually from
the perspective of students or recruits,[1] but since
in this case socialization did not occur in the
theoretically expected fashion, it is essential to
consider their actions closely.

It would, of course, have been ideal if this
could have been done at the same time as data was
being collected on recruits, but the demands of
participant observation for a single researcher are
such as to make this impossible. Therefore, these
observations were made of the training course
immediately preceding that for which there is data
on recruits. Nevertheless, it remains worth
reporting, since so far as it was possible to tell,
changes between the two courses were minimal. The
aim of this chapter is to give some insight into the
dynamics of agents who are, perhaps, all-too-often
treated as a static, cultural mould through which
recipients simply pass.

THE AIMS AND STRUCTURE OF AG TRAINING

On the face of it, the Staff College within which AG
recruits were trained, was an unremarkable training
organization. It was clearly organized into two
main departments, Induction Training and Development
Training, the Heads of which were directly responsible to the Principal, a Governor class I. Within
the Induction Training Department, which had full
responsibility for training AGs, there was a Course
Organizer who was directly responsible to the Head
of Department for the organization and management of
AG training. Responsible, in turn, to him, were the
five tutors, all of them AGs class I, each of whom
was responsible for a group of recruits.
    The AGs Course itself gave all the appearance
of being a well-organized training programme with
the stated aims:
    1.   To familiarize members /of the course/
          with the knowledge needed in the role of
          assistant governor and the teaching of
          appropriate skills.
    2.   To provide a knowledge of the structure of
          the Prison Service and its task.
    3.   To develop a comprehension of those
          subjects which aid in understanding of
          both the individual and the organization
          in the Prison Service.
    4.   To prepare members for the managerial
          aspects of their role.[2]
    These aims were to be achieved through three
methods of instruction:
    1.   Lectures and seminars in: (a) the social
          sciences, such as psychology and crimin-
          ology, given by university lecturers;
          (b) technical aspects of prison work,
          provided by tutors from the Development
          Training Department of the College;
          (c) the work of the Prison Medical Service;
          and (d) applied psychology in prisons,
          given by resident members of the Prison
          Psychological Service.
    2.   'Modules', which were inter-disciplinary
          considerations of such specific topics as
          'the inmate' and 'the institution', and
          usually organized around a self-directed
          project, for example, designing a hypo-
          thetical prison.
    3.   Practical exercises, such as the two
          'prison demonstration games', in which a
          recent demonstration by prisoners was

reconstructed, recruits being asked to
make tactical decisions at crucial moments.
Outside the Staff College, recruits spent a
total of seven weeks attached to prison establishments. The initial attachment lasted three weeks,
starting during the third week of the course, when
recruits had the opportunity to work as prison
officers or as AGs, depending upon their previous
experience. The remaining four weeks were occupied
by two project attachments which took place between
the Christmas and Easter vacations, when recruits
undertook a project designed to apply their academic
instruction to actual penal establishments. Thus,
recruits investigated such things as the 'pains of
imprisonment' suffered by prisoners, for example.
The only remaining attachment was a one day a week
attachment to a local social service or probation
office. The idea was that apart from familiarizing
recruits with the work of these agencies, and
providing direct insight into the home conditions of
many prisoners, it would also allow them an opportunity to develop some casework skills under the
supervision of a trained social worker. Finally,
apart from these pre-programmed attachments, some
recruits took the opportunities to make private
visits in their own free time to establishments of
their choice.

Despite the appearance of being a well-
organized, integrated programme of induction into
the AG's role, the ambiguities and controversies
surrounding both the AG's role and the Staff College,
described earlier,[3] permeated the organization and
management of the course. The apparent air of
certainty surrounding the statement of aims was
misleading; there was, in fact, no agreement about
what knowledge and skills were needed in the role of
the AG with which they must be familiarized, and
even the task of the Prison Service was a problematic subject. The result, therefore, was that the
aims, though clear, lacked credibility. What this
apparent certainty concealed was a continuing
attempt by the Prison Service to decide upon what,
exactly, was relevant and for what role recruits,
were in fact being trained. The course, as it
existed at the time, was acknowledged, by all those
involved, to be a stop-gap, the components of which
were largely predetermined, although their purpose
was much less clear.

The timetable and course structure were
dominated by academic subjects and whilst it is
difficult to establish, objectively, the relevance

or otherwise of these courses, they appeared more
suited to providing a liberal education rather than
occupational training. The academic material was
largely discursive, descriptive and related directly
to neither the Prison Service nor the AG's role. By
contrast, other subjects were much more definitive,
prescriptive, and directly related to the work that
AGs would do and the context in which they would do
it.[4]

There was, therefore, at the core of the
training course a fundamental confusion, for as
mentioned earlier, the social sciences could not
provide the kind of definitive knowledge akin to
that provided by the biological sciences in medical
education. Social science is tentative and
disputatious, unable to prescribe how AGs should act
in any particular circumstances. Moreover, in the
absence of a credible definition of the AG's role,
it was difficult to know how this introduction to
the social sciences could have been related to the
role recruits were to perform within the Service.
What had, in fact, developed over the previous ten
or twelve courses and was firmly established by this
course, was that the academic subjects were taught
as general introductions to the relevant disciplines.
They were taught for their own sake, rather than
because they related specifically to any identifiable training aims.

Thus, we encounter for the first time one of
the central characteristics of AG training, its
purposelessness. It was not clear what the aim of
teaching these academic courses was, but they were
to be taught nevertheless.[5]

THE ORGANIZATION AND MANAGEMENT OF TRAINING

Although much of the course was pre-programmed,
there were certain components that were left to the
Course Organizer, in consultation with tutors, to
arrange. Here too there were difficulties since the
stated aims provided no guidance for action by
tutors, because there was uncertainty about the
'knowledge needed in the role of the assistant
governor' and what were 'the appropriate skills' for
this occupation.[6] Tutors were acutely aware of this
uncertainty; as one of them succinctly put it:

> The whole course is so nebulous and we're
> training people for a role that we're not too
> sure about; perhaps the only clarity we can get
> is from consensus: we need to check everything

85

against each other.[7]

When it came to deciding what and how recruits should be taught, tutors, representing the different views extant throughout the Service, disagreed quite strongly. Two of the five tutors held, what might be called an 'affective-expressive' view, in that it emphasized the importance of developing recruits' self-awareness, enabling them to understand their own and others' feelings, and how these could affect interpersonal relationships. To achieve this they sought to provide recruits with direct experience of interpersonal relationships which could be analysed in 'the here-and-now' through unstructured groups akin to Tavistock 'T-groups' in which participants explore their interpersonal relationships by discussing their feelings under the guidance of a 'counsellor', a role filled in this case by a tutor. Opposed to them were tutors who shared what might be described as a 'cognitive-instrumental' view, who stressed the need to provide recruits with directly applicable cognitive knowledge that could be rationally understood and evaluated. They, therefore, saw a greater role for the instruction of practical, 'technical' knowledge, and were attracted to the techniques of 'behaviour modification' as a means of rehabilitation, and management-by-objectives.[8]

'Cognitive-instrumental' tutors criticized their 'affective-expressive' colleagues for advocating a view which was not open to rational appraisal, but depended upon an emotional commitment and was likely to result in 'caseworking the caseworker',[9] because it concentrated upon the recruits' personal adjustment rather than teaching a method. The criticism made by way of reply was that these supposedly rational techniques were naively simplistic and unproven. Given the poverty of such techniques, as they saw it, 'affective-expressive' tutors felt obliged to try and teach recruits how to use their own personality in as self-conscious and sensitive a manner as possible.

The disagreements about policy matters that this conflict of views generated were profound and widespread. However, although much of the structure of the course was fixed in advance, decisions needed to be made about tutors' own contributions and about those parts of the timetable, such as projects and exercises, for which they were responsible. Whilst it was the Course Organizer who was responsible to the Head of Department for the AGs Course, these decisions were determined through the consensus of all the tutors. This was for several reasons, first, the Course Organizer was only of the same rank as the other tutors, had only the same experience of AG training as two of the tutors, which itself only extended to having tutored on the previous training course, and had less seniority that one of the tutors, all of which would have restricted any assertion of authority that he could have made, even had he wanted to. Second, a more authoritative approach to decision-making would only have exacerbated the existing disagreements even further and alienated half the tutors upon whom the Course Organizer was reliant for the implementation of policy. Finally, the training course was supposed to be common to all recruits and, therefore, some compromise agreement between the various factions was necessary in order to maintain at least the appearance of integration. As the Course Organizer said, 'I can't say to /Head of Department/ "Well, so-and-so's doing his own thing and I don't know what he'll be doing next week"'.[10]

Since tutors could not agree about the precise aims of the course, they arrived at the necessary measure of consensus via informal, vague statements of principle[11] which avoided any reference to the role for which recruits were being trained. The principle, in the jargon of the Staff College, was to satisfy recruits' 'training needs'. This was an attractive formulation to tutors, because besides shifting attention away from the contentious future role of the AG and to the recruits themselves, it also meant that because of the undoubted heterogeneity of recruits, any assessment of 'training needs' would necessarily be individualized and, therefore, the different treatment of different recruits by different tutors could be justified by the idiosyncracies of their 'training needs'. The principle of individualized 'training needs' ensured that compromises could be formulated without having to raise the issue of common aims and the AG's role, about which there was so much disagreement.

Whilst the benefit that accrued from this principle was that it allowed tutors to come to some consensus, it also had its costs. Because there was now no common 'training need' that the course had to satisfy, the purpose of each part of it needed to be established afresh each time a decision was made. The result was a large measure of fluidity that characterized those parts of the course for which tutors were responsible.

This fluidity expressed itself in a number of

ways. First, ambiguity about the actual decision that had been taken was a frequent occurrence, so that tutors sometimes implemented what they believed to be an agreed decision in different ways and, on one occasion, the decision itself was retrospectively changed so as to accommodate the actual interpretation that had been placed upon it.[12]

Second, because 'training needs' were believed to be idiosyncratic, it was difficult to determine in advance what the aim of even a specific part of the course was designed to achieve. Instead, tutors designed a task for recruits to complete, usually according to the latters' own devices, and derive whatever benefit was appropriate to their individual needs. One example amongst many of this was the 'Previous Experience Project', which took place at the beginning of the course after recruits had returned from their initial attachment. The Project divided recruits into three groups - ex-officers, graduates, and changed career direct-entrants - and asked them to decide what they considered to be the contribution they could make to the course from their previous experience and what they collectively felt their 'training needs' were. The declared aims of this exercise were: to provide a report which could be used to guide teaching; a group experience different to that of their tutorial group; an exploration of felt anxieties; and training in how to organize a group to complete a given task.[13] This multiplicity of aims not only accorded with the multiplicity of assumed 'training needs', but also, and much more importantly, satisfied the competing definitions tutors had about the proper role of such an exercise.[14]

Third, and connected to this, was the tendency to leave recruits to interpret such projects and exercises. Thus, for example, in the Previous Experience Project tutors expressly avoided any mention of 'relevance' because, they claimed, they did not want to prejudge what, if anything, was relevant.[15] Did the relevance lie in the action of the individuals acting as a group, or in what they produced? Such a question, if it were to be answered by tutors, would have inevitably led to fundamental disagreements which would have prevented anything being agreed, but by granting the discretion to recruits to interpret the instructions, these disagreements could be avoided and the decision, at least notionally, taken.

However, if the course was all things to the tutors involved, it was equally likely to appear as

all things to all men from the perspective of
recruits. From the latter's perspective it was
likely that those parts of the course for which
tutors were responsible would appear to lack
direction.

TUTORIAL AUTONOMY

The problems arising from the adoption of the
principle of individual 'training needs' were not
restricted to those parts of the timetable for which
tutors were directly responsible, but extended also
into the general organization of the course and,
particularly, the tutor's role. Since 'training
needs' were assumed to be idiosyncratic, the only
person in a position to identify what those needs
were was the tutor, who alone had a continuing
relationship with the recruits in his tutorial group.
The result was to institutionalize tutorial autonomy,
because if a tutor identified the 'needs' of his
recruits in 'affective-expressive' terms and sought
to satisfy these needs through analysing personal
relationships in the 'here-and-now', there could be
little objection. As a result, the course began to
lose the very integration that the search for
consensus was apparently designed to achieve, as the
four tutorial groups began to operate along very
different lines.
   Although this issue of autonomy appeared in
many guises throughout the course, it was most
obvious in relation to the organization of the
Friday tutorial group. Each week tutors had two,
one-hour periods to themselves, one on Monday and
the other on Friday. In the past, the Friday group
had been scheduled as a 'review of the week', a
euphemism which allowed tutors to hold a T-group if
they felt able, or a loosely structured discussion
about the course if they did not.
   When the question of Friday tutorial groups was
raised at one of the early planning meetings, it was
proposed that this arrangement should continue.
However, such a suggestion was anathema to those
with a 'cognitive-instrumental' approach who had
recently joined the tutorial staff. The ensuing
acrimonious discussion took several more meetings to
resolve. The eventual compromise resulted in an
implicit acknowledgement of tutorial autonomy, for
it was that 'Friday is a mixed review and direct
teaching session and group experience'.[16] Accordingly, two tutors ran T-group type sessions, whilst

the others did not.

Once established, tutorial autonomy was invoked even in the most trivial areas, so that there was no agreed schedule of topics to be covered in the Monday tutorial group.[17] Similarly, when it was decided to reduce the amount of seminar time in the academic courses, it was left to tutors, in consultation with lecturers, to determine which seminars to reduce.[18] The result was that, once again, there was a loss of cohesion.

THE TUTOR AS SOCIALIZING AGENT

What has been said so far would seem to imply that the tutor was an influential figure vis a vis the recruits who comprised his or her tutorial group. Certainly, the tutor was the only member of staff who had sustained contact with recruits, because tutors almost invariably attended all the academic seminars. Yet, tutors themselves were unanimous that their role was less influential than it might have been, and, indeed, from the perspective of the observer it also seemed that their role was limited.

In some measure, the limitations of the role were self-imposed. Thus, whilst the tutor had considerable potential power as an assessor,[19] tutors explicitly attempted to reduce the significance of this power. The reason was that they saw it as incompatible with their other tutorial roles which required, they felt, the recruit to be open and frank with them. If the recruit believed that his frankness might jeopardize his future career, he would be reticent in his relationship with his tutor.

Thus, tutors took every opportunity to calm any anxieties they perceived amongst recruits regarding postings and reports. They also made it clear that although the reports were confidential, they would do everything in their power to appraise recruits of their content. Indeed, the whole emphasis was upon a consultative relationship to the extent that some tutors asked their recruits to summarize their own strengths and weaknesses as a basis for discussion prior to the report being written.

The incompatibility between the authoritative role as an assessor and the other roles that tutors had to perform was most evident for tutors of an 'affective-expressive' view. Whilst all tutors had a counselling role, the problem of demarcating this from the training aspect was greater for those tutors who saw their function as helping the recruit to develop his own personal resources. For example, interpersonal conflict between a social work supervisor and a recruit was, for these tutors, an opportunity to help the recruits learn more about such conflicts in professional relationships.

Tutors as Role Models

These aspects of the socializing relationship are not normally considered to be the most influential. Much more important, it might be supposed, would be the general position of seniority of tutors and their credibility as people who had actually performed in the field, which would make them influential role-models in the eyes of recruits. Here again, however, there were aspects of the role which militated against this source of influence. First, on the one hand, tutors wanted a close personal relationship between the recruits and themselves, but, on the other, did not want to divorce themselves from the responsibility for running the course, leaving the Course Organizer to be seen by recruits as the one to blame for all its inadequacies. So, they tended to playdown their seniority, whilst trying to maintain collective responsibility for the organization of the course.

Second, although tutors were obviously senior to recruits the fact that all of them had served almost exclusively in borstals, meant that their experience of the Prison Service as a whole was seen, by recruits, to be partial. It was noticeable that tutors in fact only rarely appealed to their own experience when illustrating a point or an argument. This left recruits reliant upon tutors from the Development Training Department, who taught the 'technical' aspects of the course, for 'gems'[20] about how to handle events in the field setting. The reason for this seemed to be that tutors were anxious to avoid 'deskilling' recruits by continuously emphasizing how little they knew of prison work and how much they had to learn. Consistent with the principle of individual 'training needs', they wanted recruits to be as aware of their strengths as they were of their weaknesses.

Third, when this abstention from any reference to practical experience is added to the fact that tutors had little, if any, opportunity to instruct recruits in an operational context, the authority they may be presumed to have had by virtue of seniority is seen to be significantly attenuated. Despite the fact that the Staff College was located directly

opposite Wakefield prison, recruits went into the
prison only rarely and never in the company of their
tutor. It was only in the occasional role playing
exercise, which, in any case, were concentrated in
the final few weeks of the course, that tutors had
the opportunity to present themselves as competent
and experienced members of the governor grades.[21]

Thus, although it was part of the official job
description that tutors should apply academic
content to the operational setting (which was the
notional reason why tutors attended all academic
seminars), it is no wonder that they were somewhat
dismissive of this aspect of their own role. As one
tutor said, that part of the job description was
'just words'.[22] Their de facto role in academic
seminars was to act as a supplementary teacher,
trying to explicate the concepts and theories that
recruits were being taught.

'Director of Studies'

Even in relation to actual content of the course,
tutors' potential influence was attenuated, for
although part of their role was supposedly to act as
'director of studies' to their tutees, they repeatedly complained about the lack of time available to
discharge this function. They laid considerable
emphasis upon this role, since it accorded so
closely with the principle of individualized
'training needs'. Tutors hoped to steer individual
recruits through the course by directing their
attention to those aspects of it most relevant to
their 'needs', using written essays, when necessary,
to achieve this end. However, the timetable was so
congested that there was little opportunity for
tutors to arrange private tutorials with their
tutees, a fact about which tutors frequently
complained and for which the Course Organizer
apologized just as often.[23] Hence, whenever tutors
were responsible for planning the timetable for a
section of the course, they were always eager to
build-in sufficient tutorial time.

It was, then, a cause of recurrent complaint
amongst tutors that this central aspect of their
role, as they saw it, had been devalued: crowded-out
by a timetable that was too full. However, this was
more than simply a problem for tutors, for it
exposes a paradox about the course as a whole,
namely, that whilst tutors saw the principle of the
course as satisfying individual 'training needs',
the majority of the timetable was, in fact, devoted

to lectures and seminars, given en bloc, principally
in the social sciences.

MONITORING THE COURSE

If tutorial staff were dissatisfied, they were also
frustrated, for whilst they were notionally responsible for the course, there was little they could do
to change it. Partly, this was because much of the
course was predetermined, but also it was because
the absence of clear, credible and consensually
agreed aims denied tutors any criteria of success.
In this context, the informal principle of individual 'training needs' was a positive hindrance, since
no particular component of the course could have
been judged to have been successful or otherwise,
for it may have satisfied some individual 'needs'
but not others. Denied, therefore, any external
criteria of success, all that tutors could do was to
turn to that which was immediately ascertainable,
that is, recruits' reaction to the course, which
they could justify in terms of providing an assessment of aggregate 'need satisfaction'.
     First, this could be determined by the recruits'
own assessment of their 'need' satisfaction, on the
grounds that they were best able to assess whether
their individual 'needs' were being satisfied.
Second, it could be guaged by the degree to which
recruits were involved and interested in, or engaged
by the course, on the grounds that if their 'needs'
were not being satisfied, they would be bored and
apathetic.
     Usually, tutors assessed recruits' satisfaction
intuitively and at the twice weekly tutors' meetings
would exchange impressions about how successful or
not the course had been. Added to this were
occasional opportunities for recruits to express
formally their evaluation of the course. One means
of doing so was to hold an evaluation session, when
recruits were invited to comment upon a discrete
section of the course, such as that which followed
the Course Exercise. The other means, was introduced during this particular course, when one tutor
invited his tutorial group to rate contributions to
a project in terms of their 'relevance' and
'stimulation'. After reporting the results of this
to his colleagues it was decided to employ such
questionnaire techniques more widely.
     However, it was informally that tutors showed
their sensitivity to recruits' felt satisfaction.

During the initial two weeks there was a consensus amongst tutors that recruits felt the course was 'too slow' and were concerned about the 'aimless atmosphere' that seemed to pervade the course.[24] Later on, they were gratified that there seemed to be a 'hum of light industry'[25] which had replaced this initial apathy.

Tutors could easily guage recruits' level of satisfaction with the course from the views that were expressed, but guaging 'involvement' was more difficult as it might manifest itself in either enthusiasm or hostility. Thus, the fact that recruits' had expressed their anxieties during the Previous Experience Project was thought to have proven its worth.[26] On another occasion, a tutor described with some relish a 'battle' that there had been in his tutorial group between ex-officers and direct-entrants, whilst another tutor, concurring, said how 'refreshing' it had been that they 'didn't bother being polite to one another'.[27] Indeed, one tutor seemed to sum up this attitude when he described to a new colleague that the worst thing that could happen was to be in a room with a group that was 'flat', listening to another group in an adjoining room which had 'taken flight'.[28]

The Assessment of the Academic Content

The use of these criteria of success and failure had a direct bearing upon tutors' perceptions of whole components of the course, especially the academic content, and upon what little they could do to change the structure of the course. By these criteria the academic content was judged to be neither relevant nor involving, whereas projects, exercises and attachments were.

Academic lectures and seminars were perceived by tutors as unpopular with recruits because they took no account of individual 'needs', because they were delivered en bloc, and they failed to involve recruits who were cast in the role of a passive audience. Tutors were very critical of the university lecturers' presentation of their material. A lecturer who was amusing or entertaining, who used well-prepared visual aids, split his lecture into short sections, giving the audience the opportunity to ask questions, was considered to be a 'good lecturer'. It is noteworthy that this label was not applied on grounds of relevance, since this was, in the circumstances impossible to ascertain, but was determined by the lecturer's ability as a performer.

In other words, the concentration upon self-assessed 'need' satisfaction and involvement, resulted in emphasizing only the immediate ascertainable qualities which, therefore, gave priority to performance above content. Thus, when two tutors were informally discussing why one lecturer was so widely considered to be unsatisfactory, neither made any reference at all to whether his lectures were relevant to the role or not, but concentrated instead upon presentational variables.[29]

By contrast, projects and exercises were highly thought of by tutors, for it was their experience that when recruits were left free to pursue some task, recruits were both more involved and satisfied. It was in these very terms that tutors compared the two kinds of format, when evaluating the section of the course designed to introduce recruits to their social work attachment. What was again noticeable, however, was not that the self-directed format was more relevant or more effective as a method of instruction, but rather that it was popular with recruits. Indeed, the Head of Department gave this explicit priority when, during a week-long staff seminar designed to introduce them to various types of business games and held before the course began, he said that such activity-centred methods were preferable because they 'maintained the commitment'[30] of recruits, rather than because they were more effective.

For much the same reason tutors also evaluated attachments to prisons and to social work or probation agencies quite highly. These also had the added advantage of getting recruits out of what was in the tutors' eyes the rather cloistered atmosphere of the Staff College.

Consistent with their evaluation, tutors tried to reduce the quantity of formal lectures and seminars. This was most explicit in the decision to halve seminar time in the second academic block, after tutors had found seminars and lectures increasingly unpopular.[31]

Also, of course, the popularity amongst recruits of activity-centred tasks fitted well with tutors' own reasons for self-directed projects and exercises. Not only did such methods avoid the necessity for agreeing a notion of common relevance, but also because of their popularity, they were deemed to be successful according to the criteria of self-assessed 'need' satisfaction and involvement. Needless to say, tutors showed a distinct preference for this kind of activity-centred task whenever it was left to them to programme part of the timetable.[32]

CONTROLLING OTHER AGENTS

Whilst tutors could do something to bring the structure and content of the course into closer accord with their evaluations of the various contributions to it, what was most noticeable about their position was its relative impotency. On the one hand, tutors were placed in the position of the most central figure vis a vis the recruit, but on the other hand, they had little power to control all the other agents of socialization with whom the recruit had contact. The reason for this was the autonomy that most other contributions possessed and the supplicant position that the Staff College had to many of them.

University lecturers presented the greatest problem because they were evaluated least highly and were difficult to control due to their traditional academic autonomy. Although the Prison Service paid a proportion of these lecturers' salaries, they were only indirectly accountable to the Staff College through their Professor and Head of Department, and whilst tutors thought that they ought, at least, to have a client's power to express dissatisfaction, they were denied this also. The main obstacle, as tutors saw it, was that a 'contract' existed between the Prison Department and the university, over which they had no control.[33]

Even at the interpersonal level tutors found it difficult to influence lecturers. Certainly, they could do nothing to alter the content of the lectures and seminars, even when they considered them wholly inappropriate. They accused lecturers of not adequately preparing lectures and seminars, not setting and marking essays as they were required to do, and colluding with recruits in the latters' anti-work attitudes.[34] It was in order to bring some pressure upon lecturers especially that the decision was taken to use evaluation questionnaires more extensively, since this was seen as 'hard' evidence from the recruits that lectures were inadequate.[35] However, when the matter was raised with them, lecturers' methodological objections undermined the influence of findings achieved through these means.[36]

Other contributors to the training course also proved difficult to control because of their autonomy. One such group were the governors of those

establishments to which recruits were attached
either for the purpose of working as an officer or
AG, or undertaking the two projects. Such an
attachment was inherently an additional burden for
an establishment, unrelated to its primary tasks of
the custody, control and treatment of inmates. Thus,
in permitting an attachment, a governor was, in
effect, granting a favour to the Staff College, but
because of the nature of the organization, a favour
that was granted on the governor's terms. It was
true, that in the last analysis the Staff College
could ask Head Office to instruct a governor to
allow an attachment, but since the governor was
responsible for the 'good order and discipline' of
his establishment, he could impose almost any
conditions he liked in pursuance of this requirement.
Thus, it was frequently the case that governors
refused to allow recruits to carry keys because of
the threat to security, even when this meant that it
was difficult for a recruit to, say, work as an
officer during the initial attachment because it was
impossible to move about the establishment freely.

Not only was the Staff College in the position
of a supplicant to governors, but also tutors
believed that governors felt that they and not the
College knew best how to organize an attachment. As
tutors explained, the Staff College was widely
regarded as 'fairyland' by those in the field and
lacking legitimacy, tutors found it very difficult
to pursuade governors to accept their view of what
the attachment was for and how it should be conducted. As one tutor expressed it, mimicking a
governor, 'You've only been doing this /tutoring/
for 18 months, I've been doing my job for years'.[37]

Certainly, tutors felt quite powerless to
influence the occasionally recalcitrant governor who
refused to concur with the Staff College definition
of the purpose of the attachment. The Staff College
was rich in folklore about confrontations between
tutors and governors. Thus, one story was that a
governor unilaterally decided that for part of the
initial attachment, the recruit attached to his
establishment would spend time as an inmate, before
graduating to various staff positions. When tutors
discovered this, they tried, unsuccessfully, to
change the governor's mind.

There were other, less dramatic, restrictions
imposed by governors upon attachments which the
College tried in vain to alter. Thus, although
tutors felt that great benefit could be derived from
recruits exchanging their project reports, the

reports remained confidential at the insistence of governors. Again, it was alleged that some governors locked away the copy of the project report that was sent to them, in order to prevent potentially explosive information becoming widely available.

The only weapon tutors actually had for trying to control what happened on the attachment, was persuasion, but even this was difficult, since establishments are dispersed throughout the country. Tutors visited all the establishments being used for attachments during the course of the initial attachment and prior to the two project attachments. The purpose was to try and sort out any difficulties that were being experienced by the recruit during the former and pave the way for the latter. Although, from direct observation of some of these visits, it seemed that they were cordial and friendly, tutors' view of them was more fraught with anxiety. A tutor explained that one could not telephone, but needed to visit in order to 'stir the place up a bit'.[38] Tutors also reported that recruits were often disappointed that the tutor had not visited at some other stage of the attachment so that they might have been more effective in sorting out a problem that arose. However, tutors remained dissatisfied with their powerlessness, as one of them put it, 'How do we deal with this? We visited, but... (sigh)'.[39]

In some ways the problems of controlling the social work and probation attachments were more acute, because the Staff College was reliant upon two independent services, Social Services and Probation, to allow the attachment. On the other hand, there was much closer and sustained liaison with social work supervisors than there could be with establishments. Tutors could meet supervisors reasonably easily, and the seconded Probation Officer who acted as 'advisor on probation' to the Staff College was a channel of communication. Since the supervision of students is a routine feature of social work practice, the presence of AGs was less of an oddity for their supervisors than for governors.

Nevertheless, problems arose from the incompatible definitions of the purpose of the attachment between the Staff College and the supervisors. Being autonomous, social workers were free to alter the conditions of the attachment and this led to complaints from recruits that they were under-employed, or, alternatively, being used as cheap labour.[40]

Tutors tried to persuade supervisors to alter their approach to the attachment so as to bring it into line with the Staff College's expectations, with little success, not least because of an unintended consequence of emphasizing individual 'training needs'. These had been originally emphasized by the Staff College through the careful matching of recruits to supervisors on personality grounds. However, it was evident from tutor-supervisor meetings that supervisors thought they were just as capable as tutors in assessing recruits' 'training needs', for on several occasions when tutors were trying to establish their definition of the attachment's purpose, supervisors were able to argue that it was not appropriate in a particular case because of the particular individual's 'training needs'.[41] Since there was no authoritative, consensual definition of common 'training needs', tutors were no more able to resist alternative definitions of such 'needs' than were others able to challenge their own definition of them.

In addition to these three main areas of control, there was the continuing irritation for tutors of visitors to the Staff College, both formal and informal, who contradicted what tutors had been trying to tell recruits or who disparaged the Staff College and minimized the importance of training.

CONCLUSION

What all this amounts to was a profound sense of aimlessness surrounding the training of AGs. At the structural level, the only certainty was that the course would last eight months and contain a set number of hours of academic social science teaching. However, the purpose of this eight months and of the social science content was unclear, because the role for which training was supposedly designed was equally unclear and had been so for some years.

At the day-to-day level, the organization of those parts of the course for which tutors were responsible, was also afflicted by the absence of an agreed set of common goals. By adopting the principle of individual 'training needs', tutors could agree to differ, but in organizing those parts of the course for which they were responsible in such a fluid way, they too contributed to the sense of aimlessness.

Again, the absence of aims meant that tutors were reliant upon recruits' immediate reactions to the course for determining whether it was successful or not. This led to an emphasis upon the popularity of course content rather than the achievement of any goals, added to the sense of aimlessness by its concentration upon the immediate situation within the College rather than how that situation related to the work that recruits were to do in the future.

The final problem was the inability of the tutors to do very much to change the situation even to make it more palatable to recruits. The agents who contributed to the AG's formal socialization were fragmented and autonomous, with the Staff College in the position of supplicant to most of them.

Thus, it seemed, the main task for tutors was simply to get through the designated eight-month period, doing as much as one could to help their tutees in whatever ways appeared appropriate, but with little coherent purpose. Although the Staff College had all the appearance of an assimilating institution, it lacked what may be the most crucial characteristic, a belief in itself.

NOTES

1. This is not intended as criticism, since given the limited resources normally available to socialization researchers it is inevitable that agents will receive less attention than recipients.

2. Central Training Organization programme, September 1971 to March 1972, p 4.

3. See pp 7-20.

4. During the participant observation an attempt was made to obtain a rough estimate of the differences between subject matter by rating ten minute time samples. It was found that as a percentage of total tuition time, academic differed from non-academic subjects in terms of four dimensions: 12% of academic and 49% of non-academic material was presented as definitive knowledge; 26% compared to 51% was prescriptive; 31% as opposed to 54% was related directly to the Prison Service or penal system; and 13% compared to 42% related specifically to the job of AG.

5. This ambivalent attitude was not shared by everyone, the Head of Department remarked that he was under pressure to include more non-academic content and continued, 'What they're saying, you see, is that the academic stuff is not important, when, in fact, it's the life-blood of AGs for the next 10 to 20 years; its what they can hold onto and they

need to be given it before they're swamped' (Field-notes 9/7/71).

6. On one occasion tutors were asked about a request from a student to administer a questionnaire to recruits on the aims and philosophy of the Prison Service. This was met with a hollow laugh and a denial that the Service had any coherent aims (Fn. 14/12/71). Similarly, a working group of tutors convened to discuss the 'module' devoted to the AG's role found it impossible to definitely decide what the role was (Fn. 8/12/71 and 14/12/71).

7. Fn. 30/11/71.

8. Clearly, this is an ideal-type distinction and tutors were, in fact, ranged along a continuum between these extremes, however there was a clear division.

9. Fn. 16/9/71.

10. Fn. 17/9/71.

11. This vague statement of principle was similar to the concept of 'mandate' used by A. Strauss, L. Schatzman, D. Ehrlich, R. Bucher and M. Sabshin, 'The Hospital and its Negotiated Order' in E. Friedson (ed), The Hospital in Modern Society (New York, Macmillan, 1963).

12. After one prolonged series of retrospective revisions of policy, one tutor exclaimed, 'Christ! I give a new definition of the Study Group idea to my group every week' (Fn. 7/12/71).

13. Fn. 12/12/71.

14. A further example of this was the Course Exercise, when disagreement about its aims was resolved by incorporating all the various and contradictory aims into a single composite statement. This was significant because the Course Organizer was not responsible for this component of the course, it was, instead, organized by the Head of Department.

15. Fn. 16/9/71.

16. Fn. 23/9/71.

17. Fn. 23/9/71.

18. Fn. 12/12/71.

19. Tutors wrote the report on the recruit which stayed on his file throughout his career and were influential in allocating recruits to their first posting.

20. H.S Becker, B. Geer, E.C. Hughes and A. Strauss, Boys in White (Chicago University Press, 1961, p 7).

21. During the final two and half weeks of the course, recruits were divided into those being posted to prison and those posted to borstal, and were given intensive technical instruction as app-

ropriate.
        22. Fn. 1/7/71.
        23. Fn. 16/9/71, 22/10/71 and 5/11/71.
        24. Fn. 2/10/71.
        25. Fn. 7/12/71.
        26. Fn. 6/10/71.
        27. Fn. 2/10/71.
        28. Fn. 29/9/71.
        29. Fn. 17/12/71.
        30. Fn. 16/9/71.
        31. Fn. 12/12/71.
        32. Fn. 21/9/71 and 31/1/72.
        33. Fn. 17/8/71, 5/11/71, 10/11/71, 23/11/71
and 14/2/71.
        34. Fn. 22/2/72.
        35. Fn. 5/11/71.
        36. Fn. 16/12/71.
        37. Fn. 21/9/71.
        38. Fn. 2/11/71.
        39. Fn. 24/2/72.
        40. Fn. 23/11/71, 6/11/71, 29/1/72.
        41. Fn. 17/3/72 and 29/10/71.

Chapter Four

RECRUITS' RESPONSE TO TRAINING

INTRODUCTION

This chapter describes recruits' response to their
training and poses the paradox that although they
saw their training as largely purposeless, they also
believed themselves, at least to some extent, better
prepared by it to do the job of the AG, and
considered their tutors to be the most influential
persons they had met during their training period.

THE PATTERN OF RECRUITS' RESPONSE

Recruits' response to training fell into three
stages: an initial confrontation with tutors about
the allegedly poor standards of instruction; a long
period of apathetic disengagement; and a final
enthusiasm for the future.

Initial Confrontation
When interviewed initially, recruits had quite high
hopes for the training course, which all but two
supposed would be designed to provide them with an
AG's knowledge and skills. This, half of them saw
as important to them for their career as a whole
with a further third believing that it would prove
particularly important at the beginning of their
career. This makes sense, given the fact that the
majority of direct-entrants had virtually no knowledge of the job which they would shortly be doing
and had not previously considered as a career.
    By the final interview, recruits' assessment of
the course had changed dramatically. As Figure 4.1
shows, although virtually everyone had originally
believed that the course would aim to provide basic

Figure 4.1: Recruits' Perceptions of Course Aims

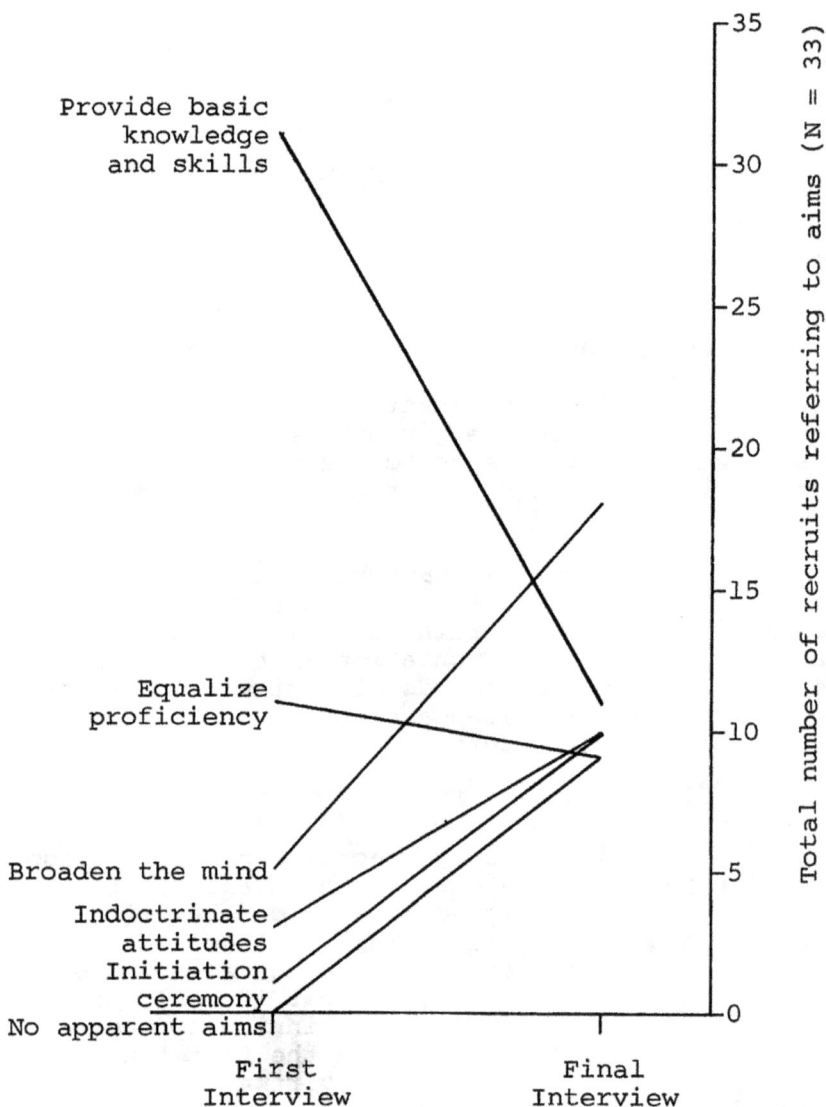

knowledge and skills, this declined to only a third
believing this to have been the aim by the end of
their training, with a compensating growth in such
other aims as 'broadening the mind'. Even this does
not fully illustrate the degree of disillusionment
felt by recruits, because there were three groups of
recruits of approximately equal size: those who
continued to feel that providing knowledge and
skills <u>was</u> the aim of the course, but who also felt
that it had failed to achieve these aims; those who
thought that the course must have had some other,
non-training, aim, such as 'broadening the mind',
with which it had met with some success; and those
who failed to discern any aims at all.

When comparing how recruits assessed the relevance of various components of the course before and
after attending it, there was a pattern of change
consistent with this sense of disillusionment. Thus,
initially, recruits had anticipated that virtually
everything would be relevant but that academic
subjects would be more relevant than most. By the
final interview, this picture had changed markedly,
for now there was a much greater difference in the
ratings given for course components and it was the
academic subjects that suffered most, with, for
example, management studies declining from rank two
to rank eleven, criminology from three to eight, and
sociology from six to ten.[1] When asked, on the
final interview, how they would alter the course,
the most frequent reply was to make it more directly
relevant and practical, closely followed by reducing
the length of the course and making greater use of
attachments and visits.[2]

Although these changes of assessment were not
confirmed until the final interview, earlier participant observation already revealed the discrepancy
between anticipation and experience. By the time
recruits started the course some of their enthusiasm
had already been diminished by the contact many of
them had had with serving AGs. These contacts had
led many to lower their expectations about how
successful the course would be in achieving the aim
of providing relevant skills and knowledge, but they
had not led them to doubt the legitimacy of this aim
itself. The result of the application of this
criterion was an attitude of assertive discontent.
Recruits frequently expressed criticism of the
content and structure of the course. They
complained about the standard of lectures and poor
instructional methods.

From the outset recruits encountered the

problems surrounding the AG's role. During the
first two weeks the problematic position of the AG
was twice brought to their attention through course
content. First, a group of specialists was invited
to talk about their roles within the prison and used
the opportunity to chorus various derogatory remarks
about governor grades.[3] Second, a group of AGs were
invited from various types of establishment to
describe their roles, which succeeded not only in
illustrating the wide variety of duties that AGs
perform, but also erupted into something of a row
between the AGs regarding the relative merits of
prison and borstal, and managerial and casework
definitions of the AG's role, as well as the
priority of custodial and rehabilitative aims for
the Prison Service.[4]

Another formally programmed part of the course
was the initial attachment, and , for ex-officers,
the pre-course training that had preceded the course
itself. In the feedback sessions that followed
their return from the initial attachment, considerable attention was paid to the ambiguity of the
recruits' future role, a realization that came as
quite a shock to some of them.

Informally, recruits discussed this point
amongst themselves extensively during the first few
weeks. Indeed, on the very first day of the course,
an ex-officer told other recruits how, according to
the AGs at his previous establishment, the
managerial notion of the role was nonsense, whilst
he himself vouched for the fact that officers saw
the chief officer as their superior, not the AG.[5]
The argument between the visiting AGs, mentioned
above, also sparked considerable informal discussion
and argument amongst recruits about the role, a
tendency that was given further impetus by the
'institution module', which was a week during which
recruits were supposed to design a hypothetical
prison. As one recruit put it, 'Some people seem to
see their role as social workers, sitting on the bed
holding the fellow's hand', making it clear that he
definitely saw himself as a 'manager'.[6] For others,
this period was more a matter of confusion: as one
recruit observed, 'I've never seen an organization
in which so many people don't know what they're
supposed to be doing'.[7]

Thus, in several respects, the first few weeks
of the course were characterized by recruits being
brought face-to-face with the discrepancies between
their anticipations and actual reality. They found
a course of dubious status as a training course

and they found that their future role was surrounded
by confusion and conflict. But what also characterized this period of the course was that recruits
were animated: they complained, they protested, they
discussed and they argued.

Apathetic Disengagement

This initial phase of the course lasted until the
beginning of the first academic block, when it was
replaced by apathetic disengagement. The reason for
this was not because the academic block was considered to be any worse, in itself, but that up until
that point the course had comprised a series of
discrete units, which left recruits hoping there
would be improvement in the next. With the
commencement of the first academic block, however,
recruits could now look forward only to more of the
same for many weeks. Despite assurances that the
second academic block, after Christmas, would become
more 'applied', recruits found that it remained much
the same as before and their apathy increased.

As far as recruits could see, the training
course was purposeless, particularly the academic
subjects which formed the core of the course during
the majority of this period. As recruits themselves
said of it: 'All this stuff is a bit too airy-fairy
for me, I'm afraid',[8] 'We might just as well be
taught flower arranging',[9] 'What bloody use is
sociology in a riot?',[10] 'They're just going through
the motions because they think they ought to'.[11]

Their reaction conforms to the pattern of
adaptation Robert Merton has called 'ritualism',[12]
that is, the use of institutionally approved means
for the achievement of unapproved ends. In this
case, the 'unapproved ends' were simply those of not
paying attention, doing as little work as they
thought they could get away with, or, as they put it,
'skiving off'. In large measure this was imposed
upon recruits by the organization of the training
course, for lectures and seminars were compulsory,
and even those periods without formal instruction
were expressly not designated as 'free time', but as
'individual tutorials and private study', because
during normal working hours recruits were supposed
to be actively engaged in work. On the other hand,
there was no check upon whether they were actually
learning anything. There were no examinations, nor
were there many essays that recruits had to complete.
The minimum requirement was mere attendance at
lectures and seminars of apparent irrelevance, and

recruits spent their time merely 'going through the motions'.

Their sense of purposelessness is shown by the fact that, when asked what problems they had had during the course, the majority replied that it was coping with the sheer boredom of it all. Eighteen said that the academic content, specifically, was totally boring, against only five who found it demanding. A further eight dismissed the course as a whole as totally irrelevant to the job and six said that the only problem they had had was listening to endless meaningless discussion.

Since attendance was compulsory, recruits felt justified in adopting various ways for making the time pass more quickly, such as reading books in lectures. There were even rules that informally governed such practices, so that it was felt to be bad manners to read or fall asleep in the front row, though perfectly permissible in the eyes of recruits, to do so at the back. For the majority, the simplest expedient was mentally to 'switch-off' and leave it to that handful of recruits who enjoyed academic discussion for its own sake to maintain the seminar by asking appropriate questions and making comments. Many recruits took whatever opportunities there were to 'skive-off', usually by nothing more than talking in the coffee lounge or going shopping. And, despite an official policy which required them to work on course preparation during the evenings, if necessary, recruits made it abundantly clear that they were not prepared to study outside normal working hours. For the majority of recruits, the main aim during the evening was to get away from the Staff College and try and forget the boredom of the course. Likewise, at weekends the College was deserted, with many recruits travelling hundreds of miles mainly to see wives and girlfriends, but also to get away from the place and the course. Indeed, one recruit said that rather than travel back to the College on Sunday evening, he had waited until the early hours of Monday morning and then travelled over two hundred miles, simply in order to minimize the time spent in the College. Another confessed that he had seriously considered not returning at all.

When in the Staff College, recruits evaluated the various components of the course in terms of their intrinsic merit, rather than their relevance to the job they were supposedly being trained for. Lectures that were amusing, intrinsically interesting, or, possibly, provocative, were valued irrespective of their perceived relevance. A good example of this was a particular lecture given by a member of the Prison Medical Service on the subject of mental illness and its treatment.[13] Despite the fact that this was the last lecture of the day, immediately before recruits departed for a long-weekend leave, it was highly valued by recruits. This was because it was clear, punctuated with interesting and sometimes amusing anecdotes and appealed to the layman's curiousity about such matters as electro-convulsive therapy and psycho-surgery. Yet, there was no suggestion that, as AGs, recruits would be required to supervise the diagnosis or treatment of prisoners, or do anything which required the possession of this information. As one recruit said as he left the room after the lecture, 'That was great - totally irrelevant - but really great!'.

In sum, for this period, which lasted for most of the course, recruits perceived their experiences as both temporary and purposeless. The AGs course was simply something to be endured, so that one might eventually become an AG and do the work of one. Most of the course had little, if any, perceptible relevance to the job and there was not even any internal examinations to act as a goal. The only requirement was that they must attend lectures and seminars. As a result, they simply 'switched-off', mentally distancing themselves from whatever the College was trying to impress upon them.

Reawakened Enthusiasm

From the depths of apathetic disengagement, recruits began once again to become animated after their return from the second project attachment, when they still had a fortnight before the Postings Board, which allocated them to their first establishment.

The academic subjects did not benefit from this increased enthusiasm on the part of recruits, for they had, by this time, been wholly dismissed as irrelevant. As one recruit put it, 'We don't even bother to see who is supposed to be lecturing now, we just assume it's another boring lecture'.[14] At the same time, the irrelevance of the academic content was no longer a matter for complaint or irritation.

Interest had now shifted away from the course and towards the recruits' future in the Prison Service, for with the impending Postings Board they could see clearly the end of the course and the reality of working in a prison. This realization produced two contrary feelings. On the one hand, they tended to be apprehensive about their lack of preparation for doing the job of an AG, and many were critical of the Staff College for leaving the period of streamed instruction so late in the course and trying to compress so much into such a short time. On the other hand, they now began to appreciate just how much they did know about the Prison Service, a knowledge which was qualitatively different from that of the layman's for whom prison life and work is a mystery.

This sense of being insiders within the Prison Service became apparent during a series of lectures from members of prison reform groups, who had been invited by the recruits themselves.[15] For the first time, recruits encountered outsiders and appeared to be suddenly aware of just how much they had become part of the Prison Service, for they saw these critics as naive and ignorant. On factual matters, they found themselves able to correct their visitors about prison facilities and procedures.[16] On questions of policy they argued that the Prison Service was not a free agent in its pursuit of rehabilitation, since public opinion would not tolerate threats to security, if this were to come into conflict with rehabilitative aims.[17]

With the Postings Board completed and preliminary visits to their next establishment behind them, recruits could look forward, not without trepidation, to their future as AGs. The streamed instruction section of the course was an intensive introduction to the rules and procedures of prisons and borstals, as appropriate. And even when staff occasionally tried to broaden discussion to consider, say, the implications of the forthcoming Younger Report for borstals,[18] recruits insisted on concentrating upon its implications for them in their prospective role as housemasters.

What the course had now acquired was a sense of purpose and so too had the recruits.

OCCUPATIONAL SELF-IMAGE

There was another sense in which recruits saw the
Staff College as irrelevant and purposeless, and
that was its failure to confer an occupational self-
image.

One of the unintended, though crucially important, aspects of socialization that has been found to
occur in other training schools and similar institutions,[19] is the acquisition of an occupational self
-image, that is, the person comes to recognize
himself as being a member of the occupation through
being treated by others as though he is one. Thus,
medical students, for example, are treated by
patients as 'doctors', addressed and treated as such.
As a result medical students increasingly come to
see themselves, not merely as 'students', but as
'doctors'.

In the Staff College there was no comparable
process. Most recruits felt they were not treated
as AGs in the College, but thought that they were
treated as 'students', and some even said that they
were treated as 'scum' and 'dirt'. This is particularly strange since, unlike medical students, AG
recruits do not have to qualify, they are formally
appointed to the position of AGII before attending
the College. The reason for this feeling amongst
recruits that they were not treated as AGs, stems
partly from the structure and content of the course
and partly from the nature of the AG's role. Unlike
medical students, the training of AGs in the Staff
College did not entail sustained contact with those
in a position equivalent to that of patients. Contact of this sort was restricted to periods of attachment. Therefore, recruits were given very little
opportunity for explicit role rehearsal of the kind
available to medical students, who, in their
clinical training diagnose and treat patients. This
was so, despite the proximity to the College of
Wakefield prison, which was rarely visited.[20]

Moreover, unlike many other occupations that
have been studied, AGs carried no very distinctive
role signs. The fact that the governor grades do
not wear uniform in prisons is a distinguishing
feature in a largely uniformed service, but was not
one that was distinctive in the Staff College where
no one wore uniform, whatever their rank. Therefore,
the only way of recognizing oneself as a member of
the occupation was either to be addressed as such or
to do the work of an AG. Since the training course
provided little or no opportunity for working as an

AG, recruits were reliant upon being addressed as such, but this too was notable by its absence.

To be addressed as an AG by subordinate ranks, entails an acknowledgement of the superior rank, usually in the form of a salute or addressing the AG as 'Sir'. However, in the Staff College, in which the recruits were the single most numerous group resident for the longest period, they were evidently not thought of by others as demanding or deserving such acknowledgement. Even when recruits joined prison staff from Wakefield Prison in the bar of the Officers' Club, they found that they were not only denied acknowledgement as AGs, but may also have experienced some hostility from prison officers. Thus it was that this course's predecessors had devised a satirical 'game' to represent the training course, in which the 'player' is instructed 'Go to the /Prison Officers'/ Club. There you are mistaken for a Prison Officer and get served within a few minutes - EXTRA GO'.[21]

Moreover, not only did recruits feel that they were not acknowledged as AGs, but also felt that they were not treated as superordinate staff by those subordinate to them. They resented, for example, being questioned by junior clerical staff about their expense claims and being told at which tables they must sit in the dining room by waitresses. The refusal, as recruits saw it, of these junior grades to accord them the respect and deferrence owing to their rank was more than a petty irritation for recruits, it was a continual denial of their identity as AGs.

Nor was this denial of identity restricted to non-tutorial staff. It is obviously more difficult for peers to confer an occupational identity, except in so far as they accept each other as peers. Although tutors went to some lengths to do this, for example, by addressing recruits and being addressed in turn by christian name, there was a difference of authority between them and recruits that could not be denied. Recruits were in a position of de facto subordination to tutors. The authority of the tutorial staff became apparent in matters of discipline: for example, early in the course, recruits were given a series of collective rebukes over several matters, from arriving late in lectures to making dubious expense claims. However, this became most apparent towards the end of the course, when a number of recruits absented themselves from a lecture which resulted in a formal demand for an explanation from the Head of Department followed by a reprimand for each of those involved.[22] All of this conveyed the impression to recruits as a whole that they were not considered to be responsible adults, let alone putative members of the governor grades of the Prison Service.

Thus, their experience of the Staff College was doubly irrelevant for recruits, since it provided none of the knowledge and skills necessary for doing the job they were about to enter, nor did they acquire any sense of being or becoming an AG. It was an aimless period spent awaiting the time when they could actually begin to do the work they had entered the Service to do.

PARADOX I: FEELING BETTER PREPARED

In view of what has been said so far, it seems decidedly paradoxical to find that all but one recruit felt themselves better prepared to do the job of the AG than when they entered the Service or were promoted. Indeed, the majority felt that they were 'much better', as opposed to a 'bit better' prepared to do the job. Also, two-thirds of the recruits felt much more like an AG at the end of the course than at the beginning.[23] All of these findings may be explicable as 'response sets': people are generally disinclined to admit that they are unprepared to do the job they are about to begin, or to say that they do not feel they are like others who already do that job. However, to dismiss findings which are apparently difficult to explain on these grounds is always dangerous, for it may lead to an avoidance of those research findings incompatible with a preferred thesis.

However, on close inspection, these findings, taken at their face value, are not as paradoxical as they at first appear, because although recruits spent most of their training in the Staff College, this experience seems to have had little impact upon them. This is for two reasons. First, the way in which they felt better prepared was largely in terms of a personal, affective adjustment to being a member of the governor grades. Second, the main source of influence was not the long periods spent at the Staff College, but the short sojourns spent on attachment.

When asked how they felt better prepared, half the replies referred to having seen inside a prison, met prison staff or been acknowledged in the new role of AG as opposed to officer. In answer to that

question recruits made comments such as:[24]
1. I suppose that whole idea of fairly strict
    hierarchy with fairly fixed positions.
    Rank seems to show through no matter how
    nice people are and at certain points ...
    and sometimes it goes against the grain.
2. I suppose I had to come to terms with the
    fact that prison officers were human as
    well as prisoners.

The other replies referred to the course
content, mainly the technical content, as preparing
them better for the job. However, amongst this
group, over half thought that what good the course
had done had been accomplished within a few weeks of
its starting or could have been achieved in this
time, and the rest had been of little use.

This importance given to personal, affective
adjustment is consistent with the large proportion
of recruits who said that they now felt much more
like an AG than they had at the beginning of the
course. Here too, the paradox is more apparent than
real: only three recruits felt they were treated as
AGs at the Staff College and then only during the
role-playing exercises. For three-quarters of the
recruits, it was on attachment that they felt themselves treated as AGs and, therefore, able to make
the kind of personal adjustment necessary. On
attachment recruits found that others referred to
them as 'Sir' or 'the AG'. Those on the officer
attachment found that they were given special treatment which reflected their status, whilst those on
the AG attachment were able to assume responsibility
for performing some of the duties of an AG. Those
few who felt that they were not treated as an AG on
these attachments complained that they were not
addressed as an AG, were not given responsibilities,
or were treated as a nuisance.

When recruits undertook project attachments at
penal establishments, they also felt, by and large,
that they were treated as AGs particularly two who
arrived at an establishment in the midst of a
disturbance and were immediately enlisted in the
task of subduing the truculent inmates.[25] On casual
visits too, recruits found themselves acknowledged
as AGs by others. It was only when recruits visited
establishments en masse that they were not treated
as AGs, but as 'bloody nuisances' and 'idiot AGs' as
some recruits saw it. As at the Staff College, real
AGs seem only to come in small numbers.

It was not only when visiting or attached to
prison establishments that recruits felt themselves

treated as AGs, but also when they went to their
social work attachment each week. Just under three-
quarters had this feeling, whilst only four felt
that they were treated as 'trainee social workers'.
Here the reasons for feeling this way were different,
for they were not addressed as 'Sir' or as 'the AG'
by subordinate staff. They felt themselves identified as an AG because they found themselves quite
frequently either defending the Prison Service from
the ill-informed criticisms of the social workers or
probation officers, or providing these others with
inside, factual information about the Prison Service.
Similarly, a third of them said that they felt they
were treated like an AG by friends and acquaintances,
since here too they would be expected to explain,
discuss or defend the Service from the position of
an insider.

Indeed, it would appear from not only these
findings, but also those of other researchers,[26]
that it is not necessarily those closest to the
recipient of socialization who have the greatest
influence. It seems that simply <u>because</u> there is
some social distance between the recruit and others,
either because they are subordinate or because they
are outside the Service, the other is more inclined
to treat the recruit as a fully-fledged AG. Presumably, this is because with increasing social
distance people perceive others in more inclusive
social categories, in which the nuances of distinctions of rank become lost. By being included as an
AG or even as a governor grade by others, the
recruit is able to present himself in his prospective role and rehearse his enactment of if.

What is clear is that the Staff College, that
apparent model of an assimilating institution, was
not responsible for recruits acquiring a perception
of themselves as an AG, nor for much of the personal,
affective adjustment that followed from that.

PARADOX II: THE INFLUENCE OF TUTORS

It would seem, from what has been said so far, that
the Staff College had precious little effect upon
recruits and that what socialization occurred during
the course took place in establishments to which
recruits were temporarily attached. Therefore, we
would expect that tutors, who are the most significant representatives of the College from the perspective of recruits, would have little influence upon
recruits, but this was not how recruits themselves

saw it. When asked to assess who had been most
influential, they identified their tutor most
frequently, as well as other tutors and the Course
Organizer. It is also true that members of the
governor grades they met in establishments to which
they had been attached were also rated highly despite the brief relationship recruits had had with
them, but this does not detract from the influence
recruits attributed to their tutors.[27]

Not only does this self-assessment contradict
the evidence reported earlier which found no common
trend within tutorial groups, it also runs counter
to other assessments that recruits gave. Thus,
initially recruits had a high identification with
their tutor, to judge from the fact that 28 of the
33 recruits said they wanted to be a tutor at some
time during their career. By the final interview,
however, this number had declined to 12, with 21 now
saying they definitely did not want to be a tutor.
Moreover, their beliefs about the qualities required
of a tutor showed a marked change, from an emphasis
upon an ability to teach, to being academically
qualified.[28] Given the poor estimation recruits had
of the academic content of the course, this identification of tutors with academic qualification could
be interpreted as a negative appraisal. Finally, it
was not tutors who were rated as having most knowledge of the Service and how it worked, but members
of the Development Training Department,[29] who taught
the technical content of the course. From participant observation, it was also clear that recruits
regretted the lack of prison, as opposed to borstal,
experience amongst their tutors.

Moreover, if tutors acted as 'directors of
studies', assisting individuals to make the most of
the course, they did so despite infrequent tutorials
which were supposed to be the vehicle for identifying these 'needs'. Nearly three-quarters of the
recruits estimated that tutorials were held less
often than once per fortnight, with almost a third
saying that they were held less often than once per
month. Furthermore, recruits' perceptions of the
use to which tutorials were put also militates
against any simple concept of tutorial influence as
the transmission of necessary knowledge and skills.
The vast majority of replies mentioned either
general, personal adjustment or discussing their
reaction to the course, with no one saying that they
discussed the Service or the AG's role during tutorials. The two following extracts convey something
of the general estimation of what tutorials involved:

116

1.   (Author: What did you do in these
tutorials?)
Just talked informally about the course;
if there were any particular problems that
I had; how I was feeling about the course
at that stage; if I was interested in any
particular aspect of the course; what I
was doing on my own, y'know, work outside
the area of the course; that sort of thing.
(Author: Did you have to present any
essays or any sort of work?)
No, I haven't been required to do a single
essay by my tutor.

2.   (Author: What did you do in these
tutorials?)
Well it would vary. Sometimes something
specific would come up, like 'How did you
get on on the last attachment?', 'How are
you getting on now that you've started the
new course?'. Y'know, it was mainly
topics of interest like that. Well, if
there was nothing specific to talk about,
the conversation would just start with
'How are you getting on?' and the conversation would take off from that into a
discussion about a specific topic.
(Author: Did you have to present any work
for these?)
Only two or three essays.
(Author: What sort of things were they on?)
Well, a couple of book reviews and an
essay.
(Author: On what?)
Can't remember really.[30]

Whilst this picture of the tutorial relationship contrasts to the general impression of socializing agents authoritatively inculcating recruits
with the culture of the occupation, it, perhaps,
suggests a clue to why recruits saw their tutors as
influential. First, it should be recalled that when
recruits claimed that they were 'better prepared'
for the role of the AG, they defined this preparation in terms of personal, affective adjustment,
rather than in terms of cognitive knowledge. It
seems that the tutors' influence may have been due
to the relatively warm, friendly relationship that
most tutors enjoyed with their tutees. Over half of
the recruits described their relationship with their
tutor as good, close and personally friendly, whilst
only four considered the relationship poor and
superficial. There was also a correlation[31] between

those describing the relationship as friendly and
those attributing influence to their tutor, for of
the 20 recruits who said they were influenced by
their tutor, fourteen described their relationship
as friendly, whereas only four of the 13 who claimed
not to have been influenced by their tutor described
the relationship in this way.

But what makes a personally friendly relationship also 'influential' (assuming that this is not a
response set), if it is also devoid of inculcation
of the occupational culture? The answer would seem
to lie in the fact that tutors represented to their
recruits that it was possible to be an agreeable,
likeable, congenial person and still survive and
prosper within the Prison Service. It must be
remembered that many recruits, especially direct-
entrants, entered the governor grades with a very
dramatic perception of the Service and of their own
role within it.[32] They were rapidly disabused of
their view that rehabilitation was a practical poss-
ibility at the level of what they could achieve,
whilst at the same time recognizing that the
problems that afflicted the Service were not easily
tractable.

What tutors did, by simply proving themselves
nice, agreeable people, was to demonstrate that
people such as they could work and find satisfaction
in their work with the Prison Service. In part,
tutors achieved this because, as already noted, they
minimized their authority over recruits, by
emphasizing the way in which they would consult the
latter over postings and reports. Also, tutors were
of a similar age to many of the recruits, with only
just over half the recruits younger than themselves,
so that informally they could enjoy a quasi-peer
relationship.

In addition, tutors appeared to recruits to be
'on their side' in the Staff College. It is not
uncommon in such training contexts for recruits or
students to see those in authority as malevalent
towards them.[33] This was so in the case of AG
recruits, yet this animosity was not directed at
tutors, but was confined to the Course Organizer and
the higher authorities within the College. Tutors
were seen as acting as a 'buffer' between the
College and recruits, protecting the interests of
the latter as much as representing the former.
Because tutors sometimes expressed disagreement with
a point of view being presented by a lecturer in a
lecture or seminar, recruits saw tutors as an ally,
who shared their discontent with the academic cont-

ent of the course.

This position of tutor as a 'buffer' between College and recruits, was demonstrated clearly on an occasion when several recruits absented themselves from a lecture and were formally required to explain their absence to the Head of Department. Although it had been the tutors who had issued the formal demands for an explanation, it was generally agreed amongst those concerned, that tutors were 'on their side', because they were seen to have played-down the affair by reminding recruits that it was they, and not the Course Organizer or Head of Department, who wrote their course report and recommended postings.

Thus, it seems that tutors were 'influential' in the estimation of recruits, because they showed that it was possible to be a nice person and still survive in the Service and remained committed to a career within it. They demonstrated their congeniality through their concern for the welfare of their recruits; their personally friendly, rather than authoritative, attitudes to recruits; and through acting as a 'buffer' between recruits and the College, which was seen as responsible for this purposeless imposition called the AGs Course. However, they did little or nothing to influence recruits' attitudes in the direction of a common occupational culture.

CONCLUSIONS

Located within the Staff College for much of the time, attending a course which lacked either a purpose or even such short-term demands as an examination, and intending to enter an occupation which was shrouded in confusion and controversy, what characterized recruits' response was aimlessness and boredom. It was for only a short period at the beginning, when their initial expectations were being contradicted by actuality, and an equally short period at the end, when, at last, they could see the prospect of becoming an AG clearly before them, that recruits were enlivened. For the great majority of the course they simply, in their own words, 'switched-off'.

The relevance of this for socialization theory is more important than it would at first appear, for the theory proposes that socialization must occur in order that a social system, including an occupation, can persist. It also would claim, that in so far as socialization breaks down, it is because of the failure of the agents to inculcate. Yet, in this case not only did the agents fail to inculcate the occupational culture, but also recruits saw the course as irrelevant in that it failed to have much impact upon them. They perceived it as irrelevant, and, therefore, refused to accord it any significance. The training course was an aimless period of time to be filled, awaiting the moment when the role could be entered.

NOTES

1. See P.A.J. Waddington, The Occupational Socialization of Prison Governor Grades (unpublished Ph.D. thesis, University of Leeds, 1977, Table 10.XVII, p 329).
2. Ibid, Table 10.XVIII, p 330.
3. Fieldnotes 4/10/72.
4. Fn. 5/10/72.
5. 5. Fn. 25/9/72.
6. Fn. 29/9/72.
7. Fn. 29/9/72.
8. Fn. 21/11/72.
9. Fn. 23/11/72.
10. Fn. 14/12/72.
11. Fn. 7/12/72.
12. R.K. Merton, <u>Social Theory and Social Structure</u> (Glencoe, Free Press, 1957).
13. Fn. 22/2/73.
14. Fn. 5/4/73.
15. This period, lasting a day and a half, was organized by the recruits' own committee and involved inviting representatives of the Howard League for Penal Reform, the National Association for the Care and Resettlement of Offenders and other reform groups.
16. For example, one speaker advocated concentrating all prisoners segregated from others for their own protection, such as sex offenders and the like, in a single prison. Recruits pointed out that such an establishment already existed at Shepton Mallet (Fn. 3/5/73).
17. Everyone in the Staff College was acutely aware of the tensions existing between rehabilitation and security, since only a few weeks before a policeman in Reading had been murdered by two prisoners on a pre-release hostel scheme. It was feared that the hostel scheme would be closed down as a result.
18. Advisory Council on the Penal System,

'Young Adult Offenders' (The Younger Report), H.M.S.O., 1974.

19. M.J. Huntingdon, 'The Development of a Professional Self-Image' in R.K. Merton, G.G. Reader and P.L. Kendall, The Student Physician (Cambridge, Massachusetts, Harvard University Press, 1957).

20. Staff College folklore has it that the Staff College was sited opposite the prison at Wakefield in order to facilitate the practical instruction of recruits. This must be considered doubtful, however, given the almost exclusively liberal arts basis of the early Staff Courses.

21. AG MAG, 1972.

22. Fn. 10-17/4/73.

23. Waddington, op cit, Tables 10.I and 10.II, p 313.

24. Transcibed from tape recorded interviews.

25. Fn. 13/2/73.

26. Huntingdon, op cit; A.P.M. Coxon, A Sociological Study of the Social Recruitment, Selection and Professional Socialization of Anglican Ordinands (unpublished Ph.D. thesis, University of Leeds, 1965).

27. Waddington, op cit, Table 10.III, p 313.

28. Ibid, Table 10.XXI, p 342.

29. Ibid, Table 10.XIX, p 340.

30. Transcribed from tape recorded interviews.

31. The correlation is apparent rather than statistical. Given the 'softness' of this data it is inappropriate to subject it to a test of statistical significance.

32. See above, pp 65-71.

33. H.S. Becker, B. Geer, E.C. Hughes and A.L. Strauss, Boys in White (Chicago University Press, 1961, ch. 14, particularly pp 289-92); and V.L. Olesen and E.W. Whittaker, The Silent Dialogue (San Francisco, Jossey-Bass, 1968, pp 161-71).

Chapter Five

SOCIALIZATION 'FAILURES', REFERENCE GROUPS AND THE SELF

INTRODUCTION

The evidence presented so far is almost wholly inconsistent with orthodox socialization theory. AG recruits, instead of undergoing the predicted transformation from a heterogeneous collection of individuals into a functionally homogeneous group, displayed little structured attitude change. In many respects recruits remained as heterogeneous at the end of their training as they had been at the beginning. Indeed, the most pronounced change was in the opposite direction to that predicted by the theory, since, having abandoned rehabilitation as a criterion of job satisfaction, recruits substituted for this no alternative, consensual criteria, and so had become more heterogeneous than when they had entered the governor grades. Only in their identification with their future role did recruits display a homogeneous pattern, but this was based upon the initial unsophisticated perception of roles associated with the prison system and was, in any case, affected little by their training.
     The evidence is no less damaging for the notion of the 'assimilating institution'. On the one hand, the organization and management of the training course did not correspond to the structured mould which would impress itself upon recruits, but was, on the contrary, fluid and indeterminate, shaped, more by the short-term exigencies of the need to agree upon some course of action, than upon any coherent notion of the aims of the training course. On the other hand, what effects socialization had upon recruits could fairly readily be attributed to those short periods, especially the initial attachment, when recruits were attached to penal establishments. The long period spent in the Staff Coll-

ege, in close proximity to tutors and other recruits, when socializing influences should (if orthodox theory were correct) have been most intense, seemed to have little effect. It seemed that because recruits perceived their training as a purposeless irrelevance, they remained immune to whatever influence it might otherwise have had.

A FAILURE TO SOCIALIZE?

It might be argued in the light of these findings that the Staff College simply failed as an 'assimilating institution', but this approach is unsatisfactory for a number of reasons.

First, to refer to a 'failure to socialize' is to make the implicit teleology of socialization theory explicit, for in order to have failed, there must have been some goal that socialization was seeking to achieve. Training courses and training staff may have goals, but to say that the social process of socialization has a goal is to indulge in unalloyed teleological reasoning, implying that training has been 'designed' so as to satisfy the requirements of the occupational system.

Second, and by the same token, to say that the socialization process is <u>designed</u> to satisfy the needs of the occupation, is to invite the question 'designed by whom?'. Here there is the implicit reification of the occupational system, treating it as if it existed in an independent order of reality with 'needs' of its own, superordinate to the needs of its members. Third, and following from the previous point, who is to say what the 'needs' of the occupation are or were? Certainly, there is unlikely to be any consensus within the Prison Service about what the occupational 'needs' of governors were, given the disagreement about what the proper aims of the prison system should be.

Fourth, even if it were possible to determine a set of independent occupational 'needs' of prison governors, it is not apparent that their socialization had, in fact, failed to satisfy these 'needs'. The Staff College had trained several generations of AGs under a system sufficiently similar to that described here for any failures to be apparent in the later difficulties created for the occupation, but so far as it is possible to determine, those who underwent this training have fulfilled their role obligations satisfactorily. Fifth, and finally, it is, in any case, difficult to imagine how a 'failure to socialize' could be empirically determined, since almost any result of socialization could have some conceiveable functional purpose. Thus, it could be argued, that in the case of AGs, their exposure to the apparently purposeless irrelevance of their training actually induced a tolerance of aimlessness which was functionally necessary for working in a Prison Service chronically beset by disagreements about its aims. Thus, rather than approaching the matter in terms of whether or not the Staff College 'failed' to socialize recruits, it would seem more appropriate to consider socialization as having a variety of consequences including, at one extreme, leaving new members more or less untouched by their socializing experience, as seems to have been the case with AGs.

THE REFUSAL TO BE SOCIALIZED

Irrespective of whether or not we are to consider the Staff College as having 'failed', it is the conclusion of this research that the absence of any structured attitude change was, in this case, at least partly due to recruits' perception of their training as an irrelevance and, therefore, to be disregarded.

If this is so, then it is a more damaging conclusion for socialization theory, since it chall-- enges the fundamental orthodox assumption that the recipients of socialization are passive and malleable. AGs showed to the contrary, that they had, at least, the capacity to be selectively receptive to socializing pressures, according to whether <u>they</u> believed them to have any relevance to their future or not. Mere exposure to socialization would seem to be not enough to affect changes in attitude, for if those undergoing socialization deem their exper-iences to be irrelevant <u>they</u> may effectively refuse to be socialized.

Two Implications: Contingency and Agency
The implications of the foregoing discussion are two -fold. First, AGs demonstrate that socialization is not an inevitable consequence of the initial exper-ience of a new role. Therefore, it is necessary not only to recognize that socialization has contingent consequences, but also the theory must be developed so as to account for the sources of these conting-encies. Second, the socialization of AGs suggests

124

that at least one source of contingency lies in the degree of receptivity to socializing pressures by those being socialized. Again, the theory must include some explanation of the sources of this selective receptivity to socializing influence.

It is to the detailed exploration of these two issues that the remainder of this chapter is addressed. The aim will be to suggest some answers to the questions of the sources of contingency and receptivity, by considering the socialization of AGs in its wider theoretical context. This will show that there are three, empirically identifiable, contingent consequences of socialization, each of which results from different degrees of receptivity by those being socialized. The standard explanation of selective receptivity lies in the concept of 'reference group', which has become a part of the explanatory apparatus of socialization theory. However, this is a concept which is theoretically unsatisfactory. When the concept is reformulated, so as to avoid its theoretical weaknesses, its application to AGs becomes more obvious. This reformulation, however, requires a radical revision of the fundamental assumptions of socialization theory itself.

THE CONTINGENT CONSEQUENCES OF SOCIALIZATION

The case of AGs illustrates the fact that socializ-ation is not inevitable, but contingent. Indeed, considered in its wider empirical context, we can discern three possible consequences of socialization.

'Effective' Socialization

The first consequence of socialization is that it may (and frequently does) occur in the manner described by the orthodox theory, namely a hetero-geneous collection of individuals is transformed into a functionally homogeneous group. It is not necessary to cite all the evidence which testifies to the power of socializing organizations to produce this result amongst those entering an occupation. One representative example will suffice: John Carroll's study of the socialization of seminarians[1] found, that despite the widespead view that religious convictions are deeply ingrained and acquired early in life, seminaries tended to produce a homogeneous religious orientation amongst their graduates almost irrespective of the initial theo-

logical views held by seminarians. This was so
marked, that the theological persuasion of the
seminaries proved to be a better predictor of
graduates' views, than was the latters' own initial
religious commitment. This study amply illustrates
the degree of influence such an 'assimilating
institution' can have.

Temporary Adjustment or U-Curve

On the other hand, the form that 'non-socialization'
can take is two-fold. The first form is that best
described by Stanton Wheeler as the U-curve effect[2]
and to explain it, it is worth recounting Wheeler's
research. The orthodoxy, prior to Wheeler's study,
was that prisons, being powerful 'assimilating
institutions', socialized their inmates into the
anti-social, criminalistic, inmate-culture of the
prison - a process referred to as 'prisonization' by
Wheeler's precursor, Clemmer.[3] Clemmer had postulated a gradual prisonization of the inmate which
became more extensive the longer the prisoner was
exposed to the inmate code of behaviour. Wheeler's
empirical test of this hypothesis found a very
different pattern. The inmates' assimilation of the
inmate-culture was much more rapid than Clemmer had
supposed, being virtually complete by the end of the
first six months of imprisonment. Thereafter, the
inmates' attitudes changed little throughout the
duration of their sentence, except for the final six
months, when they returned to the attitudes with
which they had entered, a process of recovery almost
as rapid as the original assimilation of the inmate
code. In contrast to Clemmer, what Wheeler found
was a temporary mode of adaptation on the part of
inmates which left their underlying conventional
attitudes largely intact.[4]

Nor is such an effect restricted to imprisonment, for as Roghmann and Sodeur discovered,[5] it is
equally true of that other, supposedly powerful
'assimilating institution', the army. They found
that men drafted into the army showed a marked, but
temporary, shift in their level of authoritarianism,
not, as might be assumed, towards greater authoritarianism compared to those not drafted, but towards
less. However, this shift was reverse once the
period of conscription was over and draftees
returned to civilian life.

If it is not altogether surprising to find that
those involuntarily imprisoned or conscripted
rejected socializing pressures, it is, perhaps, more

surprising to find a similar pattern amongst medical students, who not only strongly desire to become doctors, but have to compete intensively in order to be accepted in the first place. Nevertheless, Becker and Geer found[6] a similar U-curved pattern amongst medical students at the Kansas Medical School, who showed a high level of idealism at the beginning of their training, which then seemed to disappear during their studentship, only to reappear as they came to the end of their training.

Thus, in all three instances, socializing organizations which seem to be the model of 'assimilating institutions' succeeded only in having a temporary effect upon those who passed through them.

Rejection of Socialization

Whereas in each of the three preceding cases those undergoing socialization showed some, albeit temporary, change in attitudes and behaviour, there are other instances of outright rejection of the 'assimilating institution' and a refusal to comply with their normative standards beyond anything that is not enforced.

Again, this can be illustrated with reference to the army, for Charles Bidwell found[7] that those conscripts who had a professional career outside the army, apart, that is, from doctors and lawyers,[8] rejected and despised military values, refused willingly to accept military discipline, and disparaged their military superiors. To show their contempt for military values, such conscripts refused to wear their uniforms for a moment longer than they were required to, even though this involved them in some considerable inconvenience. They saw their conscription as an unwarranted interference in their professional careers, and resenting it, they resisted all attempts to socialize them into military values.

Goffman also found[9] that an apparently powerful 'assimilating institution', a mental hospital, was unable to influence all its patients. Like Bidwell's conscripts, mental patients formed an 'underlife', which was a temporary adjustment designed to defeat the impositions made upon them by the hospital. Thus, for example, whilst the hospital attempted to strip patients of their individuality and treat them all the same, inmates took every opportunity to cling to their personal identity by illicitly hoarding small items of personal property. They also refused to accept the attempts by the hospital to label them as 'mentally ill', insisting upon their sanity even when aquiescence to the official definition of their mental status would have been interpreted as a sign of progress in treatment, by the hospital authorities.

Therefore, AGs are not alone in not succumbing to socialization, but how is this to be explained?

THE REFERENCE GROUP CONCEPT

If the problem is not new to social psychology, neither is its supposed solution, for the concept of the 'reference group' enjoys an established position within the conceptual framework of the discipline. Indeed, it originated, in part at least, in an attempt to reconcile the occurrence and non-occurrence of socialization. Now it fulfills the role of an explanatory '7th Cavalry', invoked to rescue orthodox socialization theory from the evident fact that socialization is not inevitable.

In his Bennington study of the 1930s, Theodore Newcomb found[10] that not all the daughters of wealthy Republican families were converted into 'New Deal' Democrats, despite the best efforts of the staff of the College to effect such a change. Their resistance to this concerted attempt at socialization, he attributed to the fact that for these girls it was their families rather than the College staff who they took as their reference group. Since the choice was mutually exclusive, those who accepted their parents' political stance were required to reject that of the College. In summarizing his findings Newcomb said:

> In this community, as presumably in most others, all individuals belong to the total membership group, but such membership is not necessarily a point of reference for every form of social adaptation, for example, for acquiring attitudes towards public issues. Their adaptation is a function of relating oneself to some group or groups, positively or negatively. In many cases (perhaps in all) the referring of social attitudes to one group negatively leads to referring them to another group positively, or vice versa, so that attitudes are dually reinforced.[11]

In offering this explanation, not only does Newcomb introduce the concept of 'reference group' to explain resistance to normative pressure, but also exposes its theoretical assumptions as those of orthodox group dynamic theory which emphasizes the role of group pressure in the determination of social behaviour.[12] A person rarely acts alone, in this view: his actions must be dictated by some group or other, present or distant. This is because individuals are assumed to desire the approval of others and thus groups are able to exert pressures upon their individual members' behaviour. For those concerned, this approval or disapproval is experienced as a reward or punishment in itself and, therefore, by conforming to group norms they are able most easily to maintain a high level of approval, and thus reward, from other members of the group.[13]

Certainly, classic group experiments provide impressive evidence to support this view of group dynamics. Soloman Asch and Richard Crutchfield have each shown[14] that people were prepared to express a disbelief of the evidence of their own eyes, when placed in a group of others with whom they had no previous contact, all of whom said that some simple stimulus was other than it clearly was. Mustafa Sherif showed[15] that a group could impose a consensus upon a set of random perceptual experiences, and how members of the group would continue to be influenced by the group consensus in making their assessments, even when alone. Schatchter could also show[16] how groups brought pressure to bear upon deviant members, by directing communication towards them in an attempt to persuade them to change their mind, until this effort was deemed useless, whereupon deviants were ostracized and punished by being given the more disagreeable tasks.

But if this was true, how were some people, some of the time, able to resist such pressures towards conformity? In resisting they would suffer disapproval from others in the group, which they must (according to the theory) seek to avoid. The solution lay in the concept of 'reference group', which continued to maintain that individuals were pressurized by groups into conformity, whilst postulating that such groups need not be physically or immediately present in order to exert their influence. Normally, a membership group is also the 'reference group', but in this formulation there is potential for normative conflict as a result of a person's membership of several groups whose norms may conflict. In this event, it is the more powerful reference group that will have the greatest influence.

Thus, the person remains subject to group influence; the only question is which group has the dominant influence. As Hyman, quoting Thoreau, explains, 'The one who is out of step with the procession is really keeping time to another music, he hears a different drummer'.[17] Hyman goes on to elaborate that such a conception saved the fundamental assumptions of group dynamics:

> Sociologists, social psychologists, and cultural anthropologists have always operated on the fundamental principle that an individual's attitudes and conduct are shaped by the group in which he has membership and that self-appraisal and the correlative feelings and behaviour flow from the individual's location in a particular group within a social hierarchy. ... The evidence in support of such a principle is, indeed, abundant, but, at times, faith in the principle becomes shaky in the face of contradictory examples: upper class individuals with radical ideologies and revolutionary allegiances, those who feel deprived despite relatively advantaged positions, the products of an orthodox milieu who end up nonconformists ...
>
> Via the concept of reference group, our confidence in the fundamental principle has been restored and theory and research on group influences has been invigorated.[18]

Certainly, the concept has been widely used, not only regarding the problem under discussion here, but also with respect to such issues as voting behaviour, when, for example, voters are 'cross pressured' by their membership of groups whose political loyalties vary.[19]

OBJECTIONS TO REFERENCE GROUP THEORY

The notion of 'reference group' has been criticized, most notably by Sherif who complained that is 'is becoming a magic term to explain anything and everything concerning group relations'.[20] Others have argued that the whole concept of 'normative' reference group is so beset with weaknesses that it should be abandoned entirely.[21] However, to do so would remove the only theoretical construct which addresses itself to the contingent results of socialization discussed above. Instead of following this counsel of despair, two features of the reference group concept will be explored further, leading to a reformulation which, it is hoped, explains the contingencies whilst avoiding the difficulties.

The two features to be discussed further are, first, the implications of the concept's radical amendment to the notion of group membership <u>per se</u>, and, second, the problem that it confronts in explaining a person's motivation to conform to reference group pressure.

Group Membership
Merton has, quite rightly, recognized the radical implications of the reference group concept for the whole notion of group membership.[22] Within conventional group dynamics, the assumption is that group membership is an objective fact, determined by one's physical proximity to others, or, at least, by one's socially defined position. It is this assumption that justified the group experiments of Asch and others, referred to above,[23] for these experimental groups of people, previously unknown to each other and who were unlikely to have any future relationship, could only be taken as paradigmatic of group behaviour if there was little more to being a member of a group than being in the company of other people.

As Merton observed, what the concept of 'reference group' did was to introduce another dimension of group membership, namely 'felt belonging' or 'identification' with the group, and since this was independent of one's location within a group, it generates at least four types of orientation to group membership, as in Figure 5.1. The types

Figure 5.1: Types of Orientation to Group Membership

		Social Location	
		+	−
	+	Member	Identifying non-member
Belonging			
	−	Deviant member	Non-member

'member' and 'non-member' are unproblematic, but it is the other cells which deserve our attention, for in both of these we have introduced a concept of a marginal member.

The 'identifying non-member', refers to the person who is not actually in the group, but desires to be and, therefore, adopts the norms of the particular group. This concept has proven to be of value to social psychologists, because if membership was determined solely by location, it would be difficult to explain the frequency with which transitions between groups occur so smoothly. If a person can begin to adopt the norms of a group of which he is not yet a member, he will not be faced with the sudden shock of having to abandon one set of norms and adopt another set at the moment of transition. Hence, this process came to be called 'anticipatory socialization'.[25] It is obviously closely associated with the whole 'reference group' concept.

The 'deviant member' is a concept that has not received nearly as much attention from social psychologists, but is obviously the opposite side of the same coin, and the side we are most concerned with here. It refers to those who, although they are located within a group, do not conform to its norms, and, presumably, suffer disapproval and rejection as a consequence. It is also the opposite side of the coin to 'anticipatory socialization', for in so far as the norms of two groups are incompatible (which is the only occasion when any of these distinctions matter), then whilst a person is identifying with a group of which he is not yet a member and adopting their norms, he must, presumably, be deviating from the norms of the group of which he is currently a member.

In sum, therefore, the notion of 'reference group' does not simply add an additional dimension of group membership, it actually substitutes identification for location as the main explanatory variable, since it is identification which determines behaviour. Those who identify with a group, be they members or non-members, adopt the group's norms and behave in accordance with them, whilst those who do not identify, reject or are indifferent to those norms irrespective of whether they are socially defined as members of not.

But it was not this that was the radical implication of the 'reference group' concept in itself. What was radical was that having given priority to 'identification', it entailed that individuals would now be credited with being selectively receptive to socializing influences. As Hyman and Singer acknowledge:

> The group to which we give allegiance, and to whose standards we try to conform, is determined by our own <u>selective affinity</u>, choosing

amongst all the personal influences accessible to us.[26]
As such, this conception is very different to that of conventional group dynamic theory which, essentially, viewed the individual as pushed around by group pressures acting upon him, over which he had little control.

However, in introducing human agency into the explanation of social actions this view also entails the abandonment of any explanation, for this view is tantamount to an admission that people are susceptible to group influences if, and only if, they choose to be. In the absence of some explanation of how and why people choose to be selectively receptive, this concept becomes the 'magic term' of which Sherif, rightly, complains. At the same time, it is also clear that any attempted explanation which fails to accord individuals agency will prove inadequate, since people have demonstrated that they are not pushed around by the kinds of group pressure postulated by group dynamic theory.

Conformity Motivation
The second difficulty with the 'reference group' concept concerns its attribution to distant groups of influence, which is supposedly sufficient to outweigh the immediately apparent pressure of proximal groups, for it is not at all clear how this influence is conveyed or why individuals succumb to it.

The problem is two-fold. First, there is the problem of explaining how the members of the reference group know of the behaviour of their members at such a distance. How, for example, were the parents of Bennington girls to know whether, within the confines of the College, their daughters were expressing support for 'New Deal' Democratic Party policies, if the girls did not elect to tell them? If parents could not or need not have been aware of their daughters' behaviour, why did their daughters voluntarily incur the painful rejection of their peers, rather than simply be hypocritical, espousing one political view in the company of their peers and another in the company of their parents? Within the conceptual framework of group dynamic theory, with its assumption that group members will seek the rewards of approval, it is difficult to understand why an individual would not maximize approval by dissimulation.

Second, and linked to the above, is the problem of how distant groups are able to exert sanctions, even if they are aware of the transgressions of their distant member. Parents might, of course, write or telephone, or even visit their wayward child, threaten to cut their allowance or a variety of other sanctions. However, group dynamic theory places much of its emphasis upon more subtle forms of disapproval, as shown by the Schachter experiment.[27] Parents might be relatively capable of bringing even this pressure to bear, but how could the professional colleagues of conscripted soldiers bring equivalent pressure to bear, given (a) that the professional group is an amorphous and scattered entity, and (b) that the conscripts were only minimally complying with the requirements of the army?

The conventional solution to both these problems is contained in Harold Kelley's formulation that 'Social influences become internalized and operate through the <u>self-delivery</u> of rewards and punishment'.[28] However, such a formulation is unsatisfactory, since, first, in postulating a theory of 'social flagellation', it begs rather than answers the question of why individuals do not maximize rewarding approval by dissimulation. Why, in other words, would people punish themselves for complying with immediate group pressures, when they could obtain rewards from their membership group without fear of punishment from their reference group?

Second, Kelley's formulation requires that the person should, at some stage, have belonged to his reference group, during which time the group, presumably acting according to normal group dynamics, will have enforced normative behaviour and these norms will, in turn, have been internalized and continue to affect behaviour outside the group context. However, the 'reference group' concept includes referents which do not permit this. As Hyman and Singer explain:

> Not all reference groups are organized entities. They may be vague collectivities, or sprawling social categories, or groups out of the dead past, or not yet born. Some reference individuals may also be long departed. They may be living structures only in the mind of the perceiver and do not communicate or transact behaviour. Here there is relatively free rein for autistic perception of norms.[29]

Individuals could not internalize the norms and values of some of these groups, because they are not 'groups' in the sense of conventional group dynamic theory. 'Posterity' or one's ancestors are not in a

position to have expressed their approval or disapproval, because they 'do not communicate or transact
behaviour', and, if so, they cannot inculcate the
norms and values to be internalized. Thus, devoid
of the mechanism of internalization, the problem of
how 'groups' exercise surveillance over, or exert
influence upon their 'members' becomes insuperable,
since there is no explanation of why a person would
incur the painful disapproval of his membership
group in return for the illusory rewards of the
approval of his materially non-existent 'reference
group'.

Moreover, in saying that 'there is relatively
free rein for autistic perception of norms', explanation is, once again, abandoned, for this is an
admission that individuals can believe that the
norms of their 'reference group' are whatever they
choose to make them. In other words, people are
pushed around by group pressures, except when they
choose not to be.

THE REFERENCE GROUP OF AGS?

The discussion has so far concentrated upon the
difficulties that arise from the attempt to explain
resistance to socialization in terms of external
reference groups acting as a source of countervail-
ing normative pressure to that of the membership
group. This is not the only way in which the
concept of 'reference group' can be invoked to
explain a lack of socialization, as the case of AGs
clearly reveals. Here too, however, the concept
encounters essentially the same severe difficulties
as those discussed above.

Recruits were clearly not 'deviant members' of
their new occupation; they were, if anything,
'identifying non-members', for after all they did
want to become AGs. There was no evidence at all
that they had some clearly identifiable, counter-
vailing reference group outside the Staff College.
In so far as AGs had any reference group at all, it
was that of fully-fledged members of their prospective occupation. It is all the more surprising that
in the absence of an alternative, external reference
group, and the presence of a positive orientation
towards their future role, AGs did not succumb to
socializing influences.

The explanation for the failure of the socialization process, is not to be found in the presence
of reference group influences, but in their absence.

The problem lay in the fact that the recruits' prospective reference group did not realize its potential for exerting normative influence. Recruits were in a social vacuum at the Staff College, virtually devoid of group pressures from any quarter, unable to perceive what they should be doing and what relevance their current experiences might have to a future role of which they, as yet, knew little. As 'identifying non-members', they had little to identify with and, therefore, little motivation for changing their attitudes.

However, if the concept of 'reference group' can explain failures of socialization both by the fact that the group does exert influences and that it does not, the term is truly 'magical' in the manner of which Sherif complains. It is difficult to imagine a case of socialization failure in which some group could not plausibly be supposed to have exerted contrary pressure, or, alternatively, abstained from exerting positive influence.

This is not to say that people do not identify with groups, nor that identification is not the crucial defining characteristic of group membership, nor that when a group is obscure people are unable to identify with it, even if they wish to. People sometimes do suffer the rejection of their membership groups in return for the illusory rewards of some materially non-existent reference group. However, the explanatory construct 'reference group', based as it is upon conventional group dynamics, cannot satisfactory explain the phenomena to which it draws attention. If it is identification that is the crucial element in conforming to group pressure, then the focus must shift from the group to the person who is identified with it.

A theoretical perspective which commends itself in this connection is that of symbolic interactionism, for whilst the conventional group dynamic approach has long dominated the literature on reference groups, symbolic interactionism has continued to offer an alternative conceptualization.[30] However, it remains for symbolic interactionists to work out how their perspective explains the resistance to normative influence and consequent failures of socialization, in a way that avoids the pitfalls of the group dynamic theory discussed above.

THE CONCEPT OF THE SELF

Central to the symbolic interactionist conceptual
framework is the concept of the 'Self', about which
much has been written.[31] In this context it will be
necessary to restrict the elucidation of this
concept to its relevance to the problem of why some
people, some of the time, resist socializing influences.

In order for us to participate in social interaction it is a necessary prerequisite that others'
behaviour be intelligible to us. The solution to
this problem cannot be taken for granted, even if it
is not experienced as problematic in everyday life,
because there is no simple correspondence between
behaviour and its meaning. To vote, for example,
may involve marking a cross on a ballot paper,
raising a hand, pulling a lever, writing a name on a
piece of paper, pressing a button, walking through a
door, or shouting 'Aye' or 'No'. On the other hand,
by raising one's hand one might be bidding in an
auction or saluting a leader; by writing a name on a
piece of paper one might be entering a lottery. The
distinction between, say, voting and bidding does
not rest upon the behaviour exhibited (the raising
of a hand), but in the subjective meaning given to
that behaviour (what we think we are doing, and what
others' think we think we are doing).

Moreover, social actions are usually incomplete
(what G.H. Mead called 'gestures'), that is, what a
person is doing at any particular moment is contingent for its meaning upon what they have done
previously and are likely to do in the future. For
example, a person standing idly in the kitchen may
be 'making a cup of tea' which involves waiting for
the kettle to boil, putting the tea in the pot, and
so forth. Waiting for a kettle to boil is not the
same as standing idly in the kitchen, because it is
related to other behaviours some of which, as yet,
are unperformed and give it a different meaning.

What is central, then, to the meaning that
behaviour has is its subjective meaning, especially
the intentions of the person exhibiting it, which
gives behaviour its sense and coherence. However,
crucial though this subjective meaning is to the
intelligibility of others' behaviour, it is necessarily hidden from the observer who can only infer it
from what the person does in a particular context.
The observer may be mistaken or deceived as to the
subjective meaning that an action actually has.
Therefore, whilst it is necessary to infer the

other's subjective meaning in order to determine the
intelligibility of his action, this inference is
open to error.

The uncertainty involved in determining meaning
can be greatly minimized if instead of treating
others as unique individuals whose subjective states
are essentially a mystery to us, we treat any given
individual as a representative of a type of person
whose subjective states we presume to know. An army
drill sergeant will, we might presume, be being
sarcastic if he says he is sorry to a soldier on
parade, whereas a friend would be presumed to be
expressing genuine sympathy when uttering the same
words to one who is bereaved. Those involved cannot
know each other's intentions in any ultimate sense:
the drill sergeant may be genuinely apologetic,
whilst the friend may be making a gesture without
any feeling behind it. Yet, whether right or wrong,
the subjective meaning attributed to the behaviour
of the other will determine one's response to it.

Since others respond to our actions, not
according to what was actually meant by them, but
according to what they infer the subjective meaning
to be, it is not only prudent but necessary to
control the inference that others make about our
subjective meaning, as much as possible, so that
they correspond to the meaning intended. Only by
doing all they can to ensure that each attributes to
the other's behaviour the meaning intended can
participants in social interaction maintain the
intelligibility and predictability of the other's
responses which is the prerequisite for calculated
action. This control can be achieved by presenting
oneself and one's action as being consistent with
the type of person one imagines oneself to be. In
other words, since the other is giving meaning to
our actions by treating us as representative of some
recognizable social type whose subjective states are
presumed to be known, if we present ourselves in the
way in which we wish to be seen, the subjective
states attributed to us will correspond to the
actual meanings we wish to convey. This is not to
imply a cosy, integrated, non-conflictual view of
social interaction, for the armed robber is just as
reliant upon this process of reciprocal inference in
convincing his victim that he is 'serious' and will
use his weapon if necessary, calculating that this
will compel compliance with his demands, as is the
milkman who wishes to assure his customer that the
milk will be reliably delievered.[32]

In trying to ensure that one's actions appear

to the other as consistent with the type of person one imagines oneself to be, it is necessary to view one's own actions, imaginatively, from the perspective of that other. Therefore, we are necessarily reflexively aware of our selves as we appear to others during the course of social interaction. But this awareness of ourselves is always mediated by the social identities that we are obliged to assume in order to make our behaviour intelligible to others. The person that we know ourselves to be is the 'looking glass self'[33] reflected through the imagined eyes of others, and when asked to describe themselves, people show a very strong tendency to do so in terms of social identities, such as those of age, sex, familial roles, occupation and so forth.[34]

It might appear from what has been said so far that a person can believe himself to be whoever he wishes, but this is not so. The concept of the Self repeatedly confronts reality, since after anticipating how the other will infer the subjective meaning of a prospective action, the person must act accordingly - as though his anticipation was true. It is now that the person's definition of the situation - who he is, who the other is, and what the action means - is open to refutation, for the other's response may be inconsistent with that definition. This may be overt, as when a person encounters the response 'Who do you think you are?', or 'Who do you think you're talking to?', or it may be implicit in that the response is inconsistent with his definition of the situation, as might happen if a robber's victim treated the whole event as a huge joke. Where inconsistency is encountered, it is necessary for the participants to redefine the situation before interaction can proceed.[35]

Thus, we make the behaviour of others intelligible to us, by making our own behaviour intelligible to them, by behaving in a manner consistent with the type of person we imagine ourselves to be, but this is always open to refutation if the other fails to respond in a manner consistent with our anticipations. However, since intelligibility is a prerequisite of calculative social action, the prospect that their definition of the situation may be refuted is of concern to most people. People, it is postulated, actively seek the validation of their definition of the situation, and most of all, of their conception of themselves, for to do so is to maintain an intelligible and, more or less, controllable social environment in which actions have predictable consequences.

Thus, to summarize this brief resume of the
concept of Self, whenever a person acts, he adopts a
Self which makes that action intelligible to himself
and to others. This Self is, however, dependent
upon the validation of others for its maintenance,
since it is a conception of how we appear to others,
and if others fail to confirm that we appear as we
imagine we appear, our conception must eventually
change.

RESISTANCE TO SOCIALIZING INFLUENCES AND THE SELF

Having briefly sketched the concept of the Self,
what advantages does it have in resolving the problems encountered with the concept of 'reference
group' when applied to the question of why some
people resist socializing influences? It resolves
the three main areas of difficulty identified in the
earlier discussion of this concept, namely, the
nature of group pressures, how and why people identify with some groups and not others, and how and why
people can be influenced by distant and non-existant
groups.

Group Membership

Group dynamic theory conceives group pressures as
the selective application of approval and disapproval by members to each other, on the assumption
that man is an 'approval-seeker'. The concept of
the Self fundamental amends this conception of man.
Whilst acknowledging that pressures may, under
certain circumstances, be exerted through the use of
approval and disapproval by the group, the crucial
condition which needs to be met in order that group
approval can be effective, is that the individual
defines himself as a group member.
    Clearly, the majority of social identities that
people adopt to make their actions intelligible, are
those of members of groups. Thus, a person might
define himself as a member of a political party -
'I am a Socialist' - but if so, how is this validated? Validation comes from others' acceptance that
he is a Socialist, expressed by their acceptance and
approval, if they too are Socialists, but also by
their disapproval and rejection, if they are not.
    Thus, approval and disapproval are not exper-
ienced as rewarding or punishing per se, but are
dependent upon the person's definition of himself as
belonging to a group or not. Indeed, approval from

the 'wrong' groups may prove disconcerting, since this would invalidate a person's concept of himself as being unlike members of these groups. In some circumstances individuals may, and do, solicit the disapproval of those groups to whom they feel negatively related, so as to confirm that they are not like them.

Whilst it is not claimed that this view is counter-intuitive, it does oppose the conventional group-dynamic concept of 'man the approval-seeker'.

Identification With Groups

Clearly the symbolic interactionist notion of the Self is consistent with the priority given to identification in defining group membership,[36] for whether or not a person is located, physically or socially within a group, it will affect his behaviour only if he identifies with it, that is, defines himself as a member. If not, then the disapproval that other members of the group will show towards him will not be experienced as painful since it will not invalidate any part of his self-concept.

This, of course, also has some bearing upon the problem of motivation, because this problem only arises from the group dynamic assumption that all approval is rewarding and all disapproval punishing. We no longer need explain why a person suffers the painful rejection of their membership group in return for the rewards of the approval of their reference group, rather than dissimulate and maximize their rewards, because if the membership group forms no part of the self-concept the rejection by its members will not be experienced as 'painful' at all.

Distant and Non-Existent Groups

This brings us to the final, and most difficult, aspect of reference group behaviour, the influence of groups who are distant or non-existent. This is a problem for the group dynamic approach, because it must explain how approval or disapproval is conveyed by distant groups or produced by materially non-existent entities. In other words, how does a reference group make its influence felt?

From the symbolic interactionist perspective this problem arises only because of the mistaken view of group dynamic theorists about how groups exert influence, whether immediately present or not. The error is to conceive of group pressures as

objectively real behaviour by the group directed
towards one, or more, of its members. However, in
order to make the behaviour of other group members
intelligible as approval or disapproval, the person
must place himself imaginatively in the position of
others and attribute subjective meaning to their
actions. This is so, not least because the person
must connect the current behaviour of other group
members as a reaction to his preceding behaviour in
order to define it as approval or not.

Since it is physically impossible literally to
place oneself in the position of the other and view
events from their subjective perspective, it is
necessary for the person to represent symbolically
the other's point of view by treating him as an
instantiation of a type, or what Mead called the
'generalized other'.[37] Indeed, the notion that a
group can express disapproval illustrates such a
process of symbolic representation, for it does not
require that there is unanimity amongst its members
(or even a simple majority) nor is it the mere
aggregation of individual members' dissatisfaction.
When a group approves or disapproves of a member's
action, the group is a symbolic representation
concretely instantiated by its individual members.

The importance of these symbolic representa-
tions, be they an organized group, a 'vague collec-
tivity, or sprawling social category, or groups out
of the dead past, or not yet born',[38] is that they
need be neither immediately present nor physically
real. For example, an author, when writing a book,
addresses an audience which is neither present nor,
at the time of writing, physically constituted. He
cannot know, with certainty, who precisely will read
his words nor what knowledge, personal experience
and presuppositions they will bring to what they
read. Yet, he must write for some audience - a
symbollically represented 'typical reader' - to whom
he can attribute a measure of prior knowledge of the
subject, certain common experiences and, perhaps, a
degree of presupposition, favourable or otherwise.
He must do this in order to decide what to include
and what to omit, whether an illustration is mean-
ingful or not, and even whether a joke will be
appreciated or not. Therefore, an author places
himself, imaginatively, in the position of his
audience and asks himself 'If I were they, would I
understand and would I be convinced of what I am
writing?'. When the author pulls a partially
written page from the typewriter and discards it, he
has been subjected to no objectively real pressure

from anyone, other than himself, and yet it is not himself alone, but himself adopting the position of the generalized other, his prospective readers, for whilst what he has written may make sense to him, he judges that it will not make sense to them.

There is, in short, no need to be apologetic about the distance of a reference group, or even its material non-existence, for it is not they, as external others, that bring the pressure, but the person who brings the pressure upon himself. The pressure that matters comes from adopting the perspective of the generalized other and judging whether one is acting as a person like oneself should act. In so far as that generalized other is positively related to the person, this validation of the self-concept is derived from the imagined approval of that other.

Thus, the problems associated with the exercise of surveillance and the imposing of sanctions disappear, because it is not the group that must be aware of the person's actions and which brings its influence to bear, but the person himself who surveys and sanctions his own behaviour from the perspective of his symbollically represented group. The 'self-delivery of rewards and punishments', to quote Kelley,[39] derives not from self-flagellation, but from the awareness that one's own actions are incompatible with being the kind of person one believes oneself to be. This seems to be what lies behind Shibutani's description of reference groups as 'perspectives',[40] that is, the perspectives of the others through whom one views and evaluates one's own behaviour.

The Problem of Non-Explanation

It might be argued that the foregoing account is open to the objection that, like the concept of 'reference group', it fails to explain anything, because it postulates that individuals are free to assume whatever self-concept they choose. Is not the Self, in short, just as much a 'magical term' as the concept of 'reference group' which it seeks to replace?

The answer to this is 'No', since the person cannot be whatever or whoever he wishes, for although there are many ways in which it is possible to protect the Self from invalidation, the self-concept is always dependent, in the last resort, upon the validation of others. For example, a person who considers himself to be a Socialist, but repeatedly finds himself out of sympathy with Socialists will 'discover' that he is, and perhaps always was, a Conservative.

The concept of the Self does not deny the power of groups to influence their members' behaviour. Siegel and Siegel showed[41] that although reference group affiliation led to markedly lower acceptance of membership group norms, those norms still had <u>some</u> effect. However, symbolic interactionists do not conceive of group pressure in the way that group dynamics theory does, as the direct imposition of norms backed by sanctions. Instead, they view the influence of groups as coming from two main sources. The first lies in the fact that group members often find themselves in social situations which encourage <u>common</u> modes of adaptation. Without necessarily being aware of it, the individual group member will find that he is behaving like all the others in the group. He will then have discovered that he and they are similar sorts of people, because they behave in similar kinds of ways.

The second way groups influence their members is through the ability to invalidate their self-concepts as members of that group. Those who deviate from group norms will find others behaving towards them in ways incompatible with continued membership. In effect, members of a group say to a deviating member, 'If you wish to remain a member of this group and consider yourself a member, then you will need to behave like one'. Whilst this influence may be considerable for those for whom group membership is an important part of their self-concept, it is analytically quite different to the way 'pressure' is conceptualized by group dynamic theory, for it is conditional upon the person considering himself a member of that group. From the symbolic interactionist perspective, the influence of the group is <u>indirect</u>, arising from the feedback its members are able to provide about the accuracy of the individual's self-concept.

Therefore, the individual is not free to assume whatever self-concept he chooses, for he is dependent for its creation and maintenance upon social interaction. It is only through interaction that the person can become aware of himself as a social actor and assume a social identity, just as it is only through interaction that a person's concept of himself can continue to be validated. Without validation a person's self-concept would simply atrophy.[42]

If it is the case, then, that a person relies

upon social interaction for the creation and maintenance of the Self, and particularly relies upon
his acceptance as a group member for the validation
of his concept of himself as a member of that group,
how can distant or non-existant groups, which are
merely symbolically represented, continue to have an
influence? The short answer is that they cannot,
but they do not need to.

The important point is that a person must
continually validate his self-concept by obtaining
reactions from others that are congruent with the
Self. That validation does not need to come from
those with whom the person identifies. In behaving
in a particular way the person adopts the perspective of the generalized other and asks himself 'Is
this behaviour consistent with being the type of
person I believe I am?', but if the generalized
other is not available to validate that behaviour,
others can validate it by behaving towards the
person as they would behave to people like him and
his generalized other. Thus, when the delinquent's
behaviour is rebuked by his teachers,[43] or the
military officers are annoyed by the non-cooperation
of their conscripted professionals,[44] or 'New Deal'
Democrats reject Republican students at Bennington,[45]
not only is it not painful, it is actually rewarding,
for these others are validating the concept that
these various individuals have of themselves, by
treating them as they would treat those with whom
the individuals identify. Hence Newcomb's notion of
the 'negative reference group',[46] for what he
implies is that identification with the one group,
either parents or College, involves the rejection of
the other. If that rejection is reciprocated the
individual will maintain his cognitions in balance,[47]
as depicted in Figure 5.2.

Figure 5.2: Self-Consistency of Republican Students.

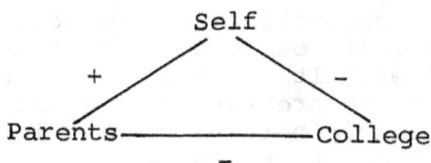

However, the Self is not an undifferentiated
entity, there are many aspects of oneself, some of
which are validated in certain situations and not

others. For an individual to resist immediate
pressure it is necessary that their identification
with a particular group be salient. As Charters and
Newcomb demonstrated,[48] simply raising people's
awareness of their religious affiliation significantly reduced their susceptibility to a persuasive
communication designed to be incompatible with those
religious doctrines. In sum, the 'group' does not
need to be present or even in existence for it to
have an effect, because it is the individual's
awareness that by acting in a certain way he is
invalidating his self-concept that motivates and
enables him to resist.

THREE HYPOTHESES

We can now return to the three consequences of
socialization with which we began this chapter -
effective socialization, temporary U-curve effect,
and rejection - and suggest hypotheses regarding
these contingent results of the process. Like the
concept of the 'reference group', these hypotheses
rely upon a postulated potential for tension between
pressures visited upon the person from within a
specific social situation and those coming from
without. The pressures, however, are not those of
conventionally conceived group dynamics, but those
of competing self-concepts.
    Following what has been said in the preceding
section, we can postulate that within a particular
situation, demands (not only social, but possibly
biological and physical) can be made upon a person
to behave in certain ways.[49] If the person complies
with these demands, he implicitly begins to validate
a situationally-related self-concept, that is, he
or she is behaving like the 'typical' ... Bennington
student, soldier, mental patient, or prisoner.
However, people are not isolated with any situation,
because they always have available their symbolically represented generalized others, and can,
therefore, view their own behaviour from other,
wider perspectives. It is this wider perspective
that constitutes the pressure that comes from outside the situation (albeit only symbolically), for
the person can compare the compatibility between the
Self he is required or encouraged to be within the
particular situation and his continuing Self outside
of it. In other words, the person must consider
whether, by complying with situational demands, he
is _invalidating_ those aspects of himself that exist

outside of that situation and to which he expects to
return.

From this postulated tension between the
situational and extra-situational self-concepts,
three hypotheses can be generated to cover each of
the three observed consequences of socialization.

Effective Socialization

This outcome is dependent upon the person perceiving
either compatibility, continuity, or, at least, no
incompatibility, between the kind of person he is
required to be within the situation, and the kind of
person he believes himself to be outside. Usually,
this will be because he actually desires to become a
particular type of person which is not only compatible with the situational Self, but requires that
the person pass through his current position in
order to achieve this goal. This was the condition
described by Huntingdon,[50] whose medical students
desired to become doctors and sought every opportunity to validate that self-concept, so that the
Self as medical student not only happened to be
compatible with, but also fused to the prospective
Self as doctor. Of course, a necessary requirement
for effective socialization is that students or
recruits have some clear, consensual notion of the
future Self. Without a clear role-image, they would
not know about or necessarily agree upon the type of
person they were hoping to become.

The desire to enter a particular role may not
be necessary for effective socialization to take
place. Less usual, but theoretically no less
important, are circumstances where the person sees
the compatibility between the situational and extra-
situational Self as inevitable, though not
necessarily desireable. Individuals finding themselves, perhaps unwillingly, in certain deviant
statuses may believe that this is not a temporary
abberation in their lives, but a permanent state of
affairs with which they must learn to live. Such
may be the circumstances which the traumatically
disabled or the unemployed face, reluctantly coming
to adopt a redefined Self.[51]

Temporary, U-Curve Adjustment
This occurs where the person perceives himself as
being in an isolated social situation which has no
relevance to his wider Self, in other words, by
complying with situational demands the person
perceives himself neither validating nor invalidating the kind of person he believes himself to be
outside of that situation. Usually, participation
in such situations is seen by the individual as
temporary, such as in the case of conscription or a
determinate prison sentence.

Rejection
This is the reverse of socialization, for here the
person perceives an incompatibility between the Self
they are required to be in the situation and the
person they believe themselves to be outside. For
Bidwell's conscripted professionals, their subordination to professionally less-qualified military
officers, was a continuing and unacceptable invalidation of the professional Self, to which they would
return. They, therefore, rejected it, refusing to
comply with these demands and often successfully
redefining the relationship on an informal basis as
a condition for compliance.[52] To have done otherwise, would have been to invalidate their enduring
and more important professional self-concept.
Equally, for mental patients to have accepted that
they were insane, would have been to violate a most
central aspect of their enduring Self.[53]

The three conditions described above are not meant
to reflect watertight empirical differences. In any
actual, empirical situation there may be elements of
all three, as individuals find compatibility between
some aspects of their situational-Self and their
wider self-concept, whilst finding other aspects
either irrelevant or incompatible. However, it does
appear that one of these three tendencies does
predominate and it is to this that these hypotheses
are addressed.

THE NON-SOCIALIZATION OF AGS

How does the foregoing analysis assist us in understanding why AGs seemed to be so immune to socializing influences? On the face of it, AGs do not
fall easily into any of the three hypothesized
contingent consequences.

Effective Socialization

Clearly, they were not socialized, since they
failed to acquire the homogeneity of attitudes
consistent with the adoption of a common occupational self-concept. However, looked at from the
perspective formulated above, this is much less
surprizing than from the perspective of orthodox
socialization theory. There was little or no
opportunity, within the Staff College, to validate a
Self consistent with the type of person recruits
hoped to become: they had neither the knowledge of
what such a person was like, nor the opportunity to
experience themselves in the role. In other words,
there was no continuity between the situational and
extra-situational Self. The removal of the Staff
College from any operational setting and the absence
of any insignia of rank, meant that recruits were
effectively treated as 'students', as they were
keenly aware. It was only when they left the Staff
College, especially when working within a penal
establishment, that they could adopt the Self-as-AG
and obtain feedback from others as to the adequacy
of their role-taking. But not only was it in penal
establishments that they could adopt the
occupational-Self, for they could also do it when
talking to those outside the Prison Service. In
these circumstances they could be the person with
privelaged inside knowledge and this distancing of
themselves from non-Service people involved a
validation of the Self. Within the Staff College,
however, this was not possible for the vast majority
of the time, for here it was they who lacked knowledge and others who were privelaged insiders.
Although it was Staff College policy for academic
contributions to be applied to prison conditions,
there was little opportunity for recruits to
perceive such application because of the limits of
their own knowledge. The only exception to this was
the occasion on which penal reformers visited the
College to discuss alternatives to imprisonment,
when it was noticeable how recruits adopted, or
perhaps discovered themselves in, the role of know-

ledgeable insiders.

Because they were largely untouched by socializing influences AGs suggest why it is that other
'assimilating institutions' are so effective. It is
not simply that those in such residential establishments are bombarded with socializing pressures, nor
simply because they are isolated from outside
influences. What seems evident, from the description of such organizations by Dornbusch and others,[54]
is, first, the importance of the visibility and
desireability of the role for which they were being
socialized. Not only did officer cadets want to be
army officers and medical students want to become
doctors, they also had a clear, albeit stereotyped,
conception of the kind of person they would become.
Even if inaccurate, such a conception allows them to
orient their actions to the future and see the
significance of what they are experiencing within
their training course. However, when, as in the
case of AGs, the future role is desireable, but
unclear to recruits, they have little conception of
the kind of person they are going to become and are,
therefore, unable to interpret and relate their
socializing experiences to the future continuing
Self that awaits them outside the 'assimilating
institution'. Without this orientation towards the
future, they tend to drift, somewhat aimlessly,
through their initial training until the moment
comes when they actually become incumbents of the
role.

Second, such organizations usually hold a
monopoly over access to these roles. This was true,
of course, of the Staff College, in the sense that
for all practical purposes the only way of becoming
an AG was to pass through the College. However, the
tutorial staff deliberately played-down the monopol-
istic aspects of the training course, emphasizing to
recruits that they had been appointed as AGs already
and that the Staff College did not have a secondary
selection function. There was also the absence of
any formal examinations or assessment. In other
'assimilating institutions' the assessment function
is often to the fore, with those who fail or drop
out being depicted as deviants, the very opposite of
the kind of person required. Equally, success in
assessment is also a clear validation that one is
the kind of person one desires to become.

Third, not only do 'assimilating institutions'
typically have this power to control entry into the
desired role, they usually benefit from the trapp-
ings of legitimacy. Military academies like

Sandhurst and West Point are acknowledged as training grounds for the military elite, just as medical schools benefit from the prestige of the medical profession. However, within the Prison Service, the Staff College was thought of as 'fairyland', divorced from and irrelevant to the realities of prison work. It was denied the authority so often accorded to comparable training establishments with which to impress those over whom it was supposed to exert influence.

Fourth, and finally, such organizations seem to provide the opportunities to validate oneself in the new role, which were denied at the Staff College. Medical students are given the opportunity during their clinical training to present themselves to patients and others as doctors and to experience what it is like to be treated as such. It is not always as obvious as this, for it would seem that organizations like the military academy, described by Dornbusch, give few opportunities for cadets to present themselves as fully-fledged officers. What the military academy did do, however, was to have a careful gradation of cadet statuses, in which the more senior assumed responsibilities and acquired rights which validated their progression towards the valued goal. For AGs, on the contrary, there was no progression, nothing to be achieved that would confirm that they were more like fully-fledged AGs than they were at the beginning. In name they were fully-fledged AGs, but in actuality they were and remained 'students' throughout.

In short, although on the face of it, the Staff College was the model 'assimilating institution', satisfying all the main qualifications according to orthodox socialization theory, it lacked the most important, though unacknowledged, features of such an institution as it was experienced by recruits. It had little bearing on their self-concepts.

Temporary, U-Curve Adjustment

In some respects, AGs displayed the characteristic U-curve pattern of response to socialization. The recruits' sub-culture, with its emphasis on 'switching-off' and 'skiving', had the appearance of a temporary adaptation to situational conditions. Also the pattern of initial confrontation, followed by resentful apathy, and finally reawakened enthusiasm, has the appearance of a U-curve pattern. However, this would be a misleading conclusion, since recruits made no significant adjustment in their attitudes that could be detected. They did not make any adjustments in their attitudes or behaviour that were other than superficial. On the contrary, prisoners did adopt the inmate code, conscripts did become less authoritarian, and medical students did become less idealistic,[55] if only for the duration of their participation in the respective situations.

Again, the failure of AGs to adopt a U-curve pattern possibly indicates something of the reasons why others do so. The most obvious reason why AGs did not make any real adjustments in their attitudes, was because they did not need to. The training course presented them with no obstacles to which they needed to adapt in order to achieve their goal, apart from simply remaining resident at the Staff College, attending classes, enduring boredom, for a period of eight months. It hardly needs saying that prisoners, medical students and conscripts encounter more significant obstacles to the achievement of such basic goals as, in the case of prisoners, staying alive.

Indeed, this is the burden of Becker et al's explanation for the U-curve pattern in the idealism of medical students.[56] As they explain, the primary problem that medical students faced was that of being able to cope with the heavy workload which they were required to undertake and the need to pass examinations in order to achieve the desired status of being a doctor. The abandonment of their initial idealism came with the recognition that the only viable way of achieving their goals was not to concern themselves with what knowledge would be useful to them as doctors, but to concentrate on what they would need to know in order to pass examinations. Their apparently cynical instrumental attitude to their studies, suggest Becker et al, was an adaptation to the demands of the course allowing them to achieve their long-term goals.

Thus, in order to produce a U-curve pattern, a socializing organization must demand that its members make some real adjustment in their behaviour which has implications for the self-concept, but because of its insulation from the enduring self-concept, this adjustment is only temporary. This was not the case with AGs, who were not called upon to make any significant adjustments at all.

Rejection

In one sense, AGs rejected the Staff College as an irrelevance, but they did not resist it like Bidwell's conscripted professionals,[57] who took every opportunity to show how they despised the military. Yet, like conscripted professionals, AGs only had available a self-concept, in their case that of 'student', which they found incompatible with their enduring and future Self. However, unlike conscripted professionals, this was not an identity which violated the existing Self; it was an identity which was incompatible with the Self they hoped and expected to become. Moreover, the Self they hoped to become was largely obscure to recruits, leaving them dependent upon such cues as marks of deference and being addressed as an 'AG'. As a result, they could not, as yet, assert their future Self in opposition to the Self they felt was being imposed upon them, for they did not know what that future Self entailed and, in a non-operational setting, they were not, in actuality, AGs at all. By contrast, this was what conscripted professionals could and did do, by ostentatiously presenting themselves as the professionals they 'really' considered themselves to be in opposition to the soldiers the military were trying to make them. Even in an alien environment, like a military camp, these men knew how to behave as professionals.

Both groups had an 'underlife' which undermines the effectiveness of socializing pressure, but a distinction needs to be drawn between the active, assertive underlife of the conscripted professional and the passive response of AGs. Conscripts were active because they knew the type of person they 'really' were and could validate it by opposition to the attempts of the military to make them 'good soldiers'. AGs still did not know what it was to 'be an AG' and, therefore, restricted themselves to refusing to be a 'student'. Although passive, the response of AGs does seem to be equivalent to that of conscripted professionals, in their rejection of socializing pressure. In short, like these conscripts and mental patients, they refused to be socialized.

CONCLUSION

If individuals can remain immune to or reject socializing influences, as AGs, amongst others, appear to have done - because they saw their social-ization as irrelevant to or incompatible with their enduring or future Self - then this has quite radical implications for our whole conception of the socialization process.

No longer can it be assumed that mere exposure to socializing influences will ensure the acquis-ition of a culture, since it must now be recognized that socialization is a process with contingent consequences. One source of that contingency lies in the capacity of those undergoing socialization to be selectively receptive to socializing influences, according to how they define their socializing situation. Socialization, therefore, cannot be conceived as a unidirectional transmission of a culture by agents to passive recipients, since the recipients are clearly not just passive, they are actively interpreting the meaning and relevance of their experiences, and any influence that their socialization has must be mediated by their inter-pretation of it.

Once it is accepted that socialization is mediated by the recipients' interpretations, a degree of agency is incorporated into the model of the process which fundamentally alters it. Analysis can no longer be restricted to the question of what socializers do to those whom they socialize, for the latter may or may not be receptive to those influ-ences. Therefore, socialization must also be analysed from the perspective of those undergoing it. Since it is the recipients who will be making the adaptations to their new role, it is necessary to determine what it is about the socializing situation that demands adaptation, and this can only be under-stood in terms of how the situation is perceived by recipients and the goals that they are pursuing.

Moreover, socialization must be acknowledged to be a dynamic process of interaction between the various participants involved in it. The assumption of uni-directional transmission gave orthodox descriptions of socialization process a curiously static appearance. Yet, the attribution of agency to recipients should not delude us into believing that they are the only participants that matter. Socializers are significant, for it is they that pose many of the situational contingencies to which recipients must adapt.

154

As we have seen, socializers should not be treated as a static structural mould, but also as active participants, trying to cope with the contingencies that they confront. One of the main contingencies that agents face is the behaviour of recipients whom they are trying to control and, possibly, change. It is as a result of the inter-action between these two participants that socializ-ation occurs as a contingent consequence.

NOTES

1. J. Carroll, 'Structural Effects of Professional Schools on Professional Socialization', Social Forces, 1971, vol. 50 (1), pp 61-74.
2. S. Wheeler, 'Socialization in Correctional Communities', American Sociological Review, 1961, vol. 26 (5), pp 699-712.
3. D. Clemmer, The Prison Community (New York, Holt, Rinehart and Winston, 1958).
4. As Wheeler, op cit, remarks:
> Prisons, along with other types of 'total institution', are usually assumed to have deep and long-lasting effects on the values of their members. The assumption is natural, deriving as it does largely from the potential effects of 24 hour living establishments that allow only psychological means of escape. The view is supported by a tendency to study the processes of induction into such instit-utions where the initial effects stand out very clearly. But in most such instit-utions, membership is temporary. Inmates leave as well as enter. If the instit-utions tend to develop sub-cultures spec-ific to the problems imposed by their rather unique character, their members may be insulated from lasting socialization effects.' (p 653).

5. K. Roghmann and W. Sodeur, 'The Impact of Military Service on Authoritarian Attitudes: Evidence from West Germany', American Journal of Sociology, 1972, vol. 78 (2), pp 418-33.
6. H.S. Becker, B. Geer, E.C. Hughes and A.L. Strauss, Boys in White (Chicago University Press, 1961); see also, H.S. Becker and B. Geer, 'The Fate of Idealism in Medical School', American Socio-logical Review, 1958, vol 23 (1), pp 50-56.
7. C.E. Bidwell, 'The Young Professional in the Army', American Sociological Review, 1961, vol. 26

(3), pp 368-72.

8. Unlike doctors and lawyers, other professionals were not given officer status and were subordinate to superiors who were not professionally trained.

9. E. Goffman, <u>Asylums</u> (New York, Doubleday, 1961).

10. T.M. Necomb, 'Attitude Development as a Function of Reference Groups: the Bennington Study', in G.E. Swanson, T.M. Newcomb and E.E. Hartley (eds), <u>Readings in Social Psychology</u> (New York, Holt, Rinehart and Winston, 1952).

11. Ibid, p 224.

12. The theoretical origins of 'reference group' theory are arguable, Urry, for example, locates them firmly within symbolic interactionism. See J. Urry, <u>Reference Groups and the Theory of Revolution</u> (London, Routledge, 1973).

13. For a general review of group conformity theory see P.F. Secord and C.W. Backman, <u>Social Psychology</u> (2nd edn., New York, McGraw-Hill, 1974). For an exposition of the 'need for affiliation', see J.L. Freedman, D.O. Sears and J.M. Carlsmith, <u>Social Psychology</u> (4th edn., Englewood Cliffs, Prentice Hall, 1981).

14. S. Asch, 'Studies of Independence and Conformity: a Minority of One Against a Unanimous Majority', <u>Psychological Monographs</u>, 1956, vol. 70, no. 9; R.S. Crutchfield, 'Conformity and Character', <u>American Psychologist</u>, 1955, vol. 10 (3), pp 191-98.

15. M. Sherif, <u>An Outline of Social Psychology</u> (New York, Harper and Row, 1948).

16. S. Schatchter, 'Deviation, Rejection and Communication', <u>Journal of Abnormal and Social Psychology</u>, 1951, vol. 46 (2), pp 190-207.

17. H.H. Hyman and E. Singer (eds), <u>Readings in Reference Group Theory and Research</u> (New York, Free Press, 1968, p 6).

18. Ibid, p 3.

19. P.F. Lazarsfeld, B. Berelson and H. Gaudet, <u>The People's Choice</u> (New York, Columbia University Press, 1948).

20. M. Sherif, 'The Concept of Reference Groups in Human Relations' in M. Sherif and M.O. Wilson (eds), <u>Group Relations at the Crossroads</u> (New York, Harper and Row, 1953, p 204).

21. E. Singer, 'Reference Groups and Social Evaluations' in M. Rosenberg and R.H. Turner (eds), <u>Social Psychology: Sociological Perspectives</u> (New York, Basic Books, 1981).

22. R.K. Merton, <u>Social Theory and Social</u>

Structure (Glencoe, Free Press, 1957, pp 281-97).

23. Asch, op cit; Crutchfield, op cit; Sherif, An Outline..., op cit; Schatchter, op cit.

24. This is a simplified, diagramatic representation of Merton's categories, for fuller details see Merton, op cit.

25. Ibid, pp 265-8.

26. Op cit, pp 6-7 (emphasis added).

27. Op cit.

28. H.H. Kelley, 'Two Functions of Reference Groups' in G.E. Swanson, et al, op cit.

29. Hyman and Singer, op cit, p 17.

30. Urry, op cit.

31. The classic account of the Self is, of course, contained in G.H. Mead, Mind, Self and Society (ed. C. Morris, Chicago University Press, 1934). Amongst recent commentaries see, K. Gergen, The Concept of Self (New York, Holt, Rinehart and Winston, 1971); J.P. Hewitt, Self and Society (Boston, Allyn and Bacon, 1976); J.M. Charon, Symbolic Interactionism (Englewood Cliffs, Prentice Hall, 1979); H. Blumer, Symbolic Interactionism (Englewood Cliffs, Prentice Hall, 1969); A.M. Rose, 'A Systematic Summary of Symbolic Interaction', and H. Blumer, 'Society as Symbolic Interaction', both in A.M. Rose (ed), Social Behaviour and Social Process (London, Routledge, 1962).

32. For a fuller explanation of 'role-taking', see R.H. Turner, 'Role-Taking: Process Versus Conformity', in Rose (ed), op cit.

33. C.H. Cooley, Human Nature and the Social Order (New York, Scibner, 1902).

34. M.H. Kuhn and T.S. McPartland, 'An Empirical Investigation of Self-Attitudes', American Sociological Review, 1954, vol. 19 (1), pp 68-76.

35. Redefinition need not be either agreed between the parties or accurate, provided that each is able to make the other's behaviour intelligible Moreover, redefinition may be retrospective, see, for example, H. Garfinkel, 'Conditions of Successful Degradation Ceremonies', American Journal of Sociology, 1956, vol. 61 (2), pp 420-24.

36. Other researchers interested in group behaviour now also stress identification as the main defining criterion. See, H. Tajfel, Human Groups and Social Categories (Cambridge University Press, 1981, ch. 11).

37. Op cit, pp 152-64.

38. Hyman and Singer, op cit, p 17.

39. Loc cit.

40. T. Shibutani, 'Reference Groups and Social

Control', in Rose (ed), op cit.

41. A.E. Siegel and S. Siegel, 'Reference Groups, Membership Groups, and Attitude Change', <u>Journal of Abnormal and Social Psychology</u>, 1957, vol. 55 (3), pp 360-64.

42. Extreme social isolation is thought to have this effect, as in the case of lone sailors.

43. D. Hargreaves, <u>Social Relations in a Secondary School</u> (London, Routledge, 1967; P. Willis, <u>Learning to Labour</u> (London, Saxon House, 1977).

44. Bidwell, op cit.

45. Newcomb, op cit.

46. Ibid.

47. F. Heider, <u>The Psychology of Interpersonal Relations</u> (New York, Wiley, 1958); L. Festinger, <u>A Theory of Cognitive Dissonance</u> (New York, Harper and Row, 1957).

48. W.W. Charters Jr. and T.M. Newcomb, 'Some Attitudinal Effects of Experimentally Increased Salience of a Membership Group', in E.E. Maccoby, T.M. Newcomb and E.L. Hartley (eds), <u>Readings in Social Psychology</u> (3rd edn., New York, Holt, Rinehart and Winston, 1958).

49. H.S. Becker, 'Personal Change in Adult Life', <u>Sociometry</u>, 1964, vol. 27 (1), pp 40-53; H.S. Becker, 'The Self and Adult Socialization', in E. Norbeck, D. Price-Williams and W. McCord (eds), <u>The Study of Personality: an Interdisciplinary Appraisal</u> (New York, Holt, Rinehart and Winston, 1968).

50. Op cit.

51. B. Cogswell, 'Rehabilitation of the Paraplegic: Processes of Socialization', <u>Sociological Inquiry</u>, 1967, vol. 37 (1), pp 11-26; C. Murray Parkes, <u>Bereavement</u> (Harmondsworth, Penguin, 1972); A. Finlayson and J. McEwen, <u>Coronary Heart Disease and Patterns of Living</u> (London, Croom Helm, 1977).

52. Op cit.

53. Goffman, op cit.

54. S.M. Dornbusch, 'The Military Academy as an Assimilating Institution', <u>Social Forces</u>, 1955, vol. 33 (2), pp 316-21.

55. Wheeler, op cit; Roghmann and Sodeur, op cit; and Becker and Geer, op cit.

56. Becker <u>et al</u>, op cit.

57. Bidwell, op cit.

Chapter Six

SUMMARY AND CONCLUSIONS

Throughout this book the underlying theme has been that of the effects of role ambiguity upon the socialization process. Compared to other occupations into which similar research has been conducted, AGs have a peculiarly ambiguous role image. Individual AGs in particular penal establishments may suffer little confusion about what they are expected to do, but, when viewed collectively, the diversity of the AGs' duties in various establishments militates against any attempt to reduce the role to a common set of prescriptions. This, of course, is not, in itself, a sufficient basis for distinguishing the AG's role from that of others; army officers, for example, perform a wide variety of duties in various settings, but their role could hardly be described as ambiguous. There are two additional factors which imbue the AG's role with ambiguity. On the one hand, its virtual invisibility to those outside the Prison Service from whom, at least some, AGs are recruited, means that few recruits will even have known of the role's existence before joining. On the other hand, even those within the Prison Service share no clear, consensual image of the AG, because of the historical difficulties in deciding what position AGs occupy within the Service. There have been disputes about whether the position of AG is a role or a rank, and whether he should be seen as a social caseworker or a manager. There has also been the structural ambiguity arising from the separation of the AG housemaster from the borstal system and the diffusion of that role throughout the Service, without any clear notion of how it was to be transplanted into the wider organizational environment.

The effect of this ambiguity was felt throughout the socialization process. Initially, it had a

profound effect upon the recruitment of AGs, for
neither candidates nor selectors had any very clear
notion of the role for which they were applying or
choosing candidates, and, therefore, were unclear
about the selection criteria. Direct entrants said
that they had not known about and had never
considered becoming an AG before seeing the advertisement in the press and, therefore, had little
opportunity to develop a coherent notion of the kind
of person an AG was. Even ex-officers, drawn from a
wide variety of penal establishments, would have
gained equally varied ideas of the AG's role, had
they developed any idea at all. For most ex-
officers, it was the prospect of promotion, with its
concommitant improvements in working conditions,
both intrinsic and extrinsic, that was the main
motivating force. Equally, selectors were denied
any clear notion of the kind of person they should
select, because the formal selection criteria lacked
credibility as a result of their frequent changes in
the recent past. The informal selection criteria
that appeared to direct, or at least were used to
justify, preferences, were arguably vague and
certainly subjective assessments of generalized
personality characteristics. As a result of the
largely fortuitous process of choice by applicants
and the indeterminate pattern of selection, those
recruited were a very heterogeneous collection of
individuals.

This heterogeneity had important implications
for the socialization process, for it placed a
greater burden upon Staff College tutors than on the
staff of those assimilating institutions that other
research has described. When recruits are differ-
entially attracted to an occupation and selectors
have clear and consensual criteria for choosing
amongst applicants, those who enter will tend to be
relatively homogeneous before socialization begins.
Therefore, some of the homogenizing process has been
achieved before any socialization is brought to bear.
Even when recruits share inaccurate conceptions of
their future role, socializing agents have the
benefit of being able to conceive of the 'typical
recruit', and act accordingly. However, in the case
of AGs, little of the homogenizing aspect of socialization was catered for through selective recruitment and the heterogeneity which agents faced denied
any simple means of defining the 'typical recruit',
indeed tutors made a virtue out of necessity by
using the heterogeneity of recruits justify their
decisions in terms of <u>individualized</u> training needs.

The effect of role ambiguity upon socializing agents was not restricted to this alone, however, for had they a clear and consensual notion of the role for which they were training, even an inaccurate one, they might still have exerted considerable socializing influence. The fact that tutors did not have a shared conception of the role of the AG, and indeed fundamentally disagreed about it, influenced the organization and management of the training course. Unable to agree about the purpose of the course, they turned to what they could, indeed, must agree upon, how the course was to be organized. Under the informal principle of 'individualized training needs' they took a series of more or less isolated decisions, which culminated in a course characterized by a lack of coherence. Tutorial autonomy was effectively institutionalized as a way of avoiding the need to agree a common policy upon how tutorial groups were to operate. However, this meant that there was no longer a common course which all recruits followed, but four more or less discrete courses, according to the tutorial group to which the recruit happened to be allocated. To add to the sense of incoherence, the decision-making process was often so indeterminate that recruits were left with little clear guidance about the purpose of components of the course.

It was this lack of purpose which impressed itself most upon the recruits themselves. Without a clear notion of the role they were to fulfill, they were unable to relate their training to the future. Moreover, since the only identifiable characteristic of being an AG was to be addressed as such by others, and this was not forthcoming within the Staff College, their experiences tended to be doubly irrelevant. The only times they felt that they were treated as AGs was during their few short attachments to penal establishments and occasional meetings with others outside the Service. For the remainder of their training, the time spent in the Staff College represented a period to be endured and, having no other significance than this, it appeared to have little impact upon their attitudes. Certainly, AGs were attitudinally as heterogeneous by the end of the course as they had been at the beginning, if not more so.

The conclusion, then, is that role ambiguity is an important factor in the success or failure of socialization: when it is present, socialization is inhibited. This is not simply, as orthodox theorists might argue, because under such conditions

recruits cannot be taught the prescriptions attached
to the role, for only rarely are such prescriptions
consciously known to recruits entering, or agents
socializing for, an unambiguous role. The significance of an unambiguous role lies in its giving
recruits meaning and significance for their socializing experiences. As Olesen and Whittaker argue,
in their study of nurses, students are able to adopt
the stereotyped role when they feel they are 'on
stage' before staff, patients, or other members of
the public. They can self-consciously pretend to be
what they feel they have yet to become. In so doing,
they actually gain experience of what it is like to
be a member of the occupation, through the process
of self-validation and, thereby, begin to actually
become, in this case, a nurse. Every time they act
as if they are a nurse, they gain more tacit knowledge of being a nurse and become less reliant upon
the stereotyped role for interpreting their own and
the actions of others. As they relinquish this
dependence upon the stereotyped role, they also
become less self-conscious of their adoption of the
role and incorporate it into their conception of
themselves. In short, they have now <u>become</u> nurses.

Faced with an ambiguous role, AG recruits could
not take advantage of such a process. First, even
if they were, at any time, 'on stage' they could not
have known it, for outside of the operational
context, there was no way of knowing when they were
expected to behave as AGs rather than an amorphous
collection of individuals, if not 'students'. It
was not only that much of the training course had no
ostensible connection with the role, but also that
what little was known of the AG's role was context-
specific and could not be generalized beyond the
operational setting. This is unlike, say, army
officer cadets, who do know what is involved in
being an army officer outside of the narrow combat
context, for being militaristic shows itself in all
kinds of contexts.

Second, even if AG recruits had known that
others expected them to behave as AGs, they still
would have had little idea about what that would
entail. Again, army officer cadets provide a good
counter example, for they know that they are
expected to exhibit 'military bearing' when 'on
stage', even when performing such ostensibly non-
military duties as serving drinks to the Commandant's
visitors at a formal reception. Should an AG be
smart in this fashion, or should he adopt the
slightly schoolmasterish attire of an ageing sports-

jacket, patched at the elbows? There was no answer
to this, or a host of other more or less trivial
questions, because there simply was no well defined
image of the 'typical AG'. Thus, outside of the
operational context, actually doing the work of the
AG and acknowledged in that role, recruits had no
opportunity to <u>be</u>, or even pretend to be, an AG.

The only identity available to recruits whilst
in the Staff College was that of 'student' and this
was perceived by them as incompatible with being an
AG. It was in large measure, because of this
perceived incompatibility that they rejected their
experiences in the Staff College, which they saw as
an irrelevance to be disregarded. The training
course became something to be endured until the time
came to enter the operational setting and actually
become an AG in more than name only.

IMPLICATIONS

There are two wider implications of this research,
the first theoretical and the second practical. The
first, and sociologically most important, is its
implications for socialization theory as a whole.
AGs show, above all else, that socialization is a
process with contingent consequences which cannot be
assumed inevitably to occur. Moreover, if the
explanation of why AGs remained so immune to socializing influence is correct, that contingency cannot
simply be written off as a socialization 'failure'.
Socialization 'failed' in this case, because those
undergoing it could see no purpose in their
experiences. Recruits were not passive, malleable
recipients of socializing pressures directed at them
by external agents, they were actively engaged in
trying to make their experiences intelligible. How
they interpreted those experiences had a profound
effect upon their socialization. An unambiguous
role is not something into which new entrants are
fashioned by others, but is something that new
entrants can use as a resource in making their
initial experiences intelligible and controlling
their interaction with others.

The assertion of individual agency is not new
in sociology, but it would seem to be in need of
being reasserted, especially in the area of socialization theory, where the 'wholly socialized man'
remains as a powerful theoretical assumption.
However, if we are really to begin to understand how
people come to acquire their social characteristics

we must concentrate not only upon the pressures that are brought to bear, but also upon how those pressures are mediated by those entering new roles. There can be little doubt that people are selectively receptive to such influences and it has been argued that their acceptance or rejection of such pressures depend upon the perceived continuity between the situational and extra-situational Self.

The second implication is not divorced from these theoretical issues, for the image of the 'wholly socialized man' can be discerned in the importance commonly attached to training as a means of changing the way members of certain occupations perform their role. If we wish policemen to be more sensitive in their dealings with ethnic minorities, or doctors to be more attentive to the ethical implications of their work, then the call from many quarters is to improve training. The assumption lying behind such a prescription is that in training policemen, doctors and others, they can have their attitudes modelled along whatever lines seem appropriate. The implications of research reported above is that people are not nearly so malleable as this prescription supposes. We need to consider training courses not only from the point of view of their aims, but also from the perspective of those being trained. We need to consider how such courses are perceived as creating obstacles, both intentionally and unintentionally, to the achievement of new entrants' goals and what resources, material and symbolic, are available to overcome these obstacles. If the situation, as it is encountered by new entrants, is inconsistent with the formal aims of the course, it is unlikely that these goals will be achieved. New entrants will adapt to the actual obstacles they encounter, such as the need for policemen to authoritatively control potentially conflictual relationships, rather than merely conforming to the good intentions of those who devise a training programme.

This seems to be all the more important for training courses in the 'human relations' and 'caring professions' for two reasons. First, the role to be filled in such occupations requires more than the mastery of objective, technical skills. A Research chemist, for example, is <u>being</u> a research chemist when he is employing the requisite skills and knowledge, but social workers, health visitors, and many others in similar occupations, are, like AGs, only able to occupy their role when they have <u>become</u> the type of person predicated by their role.

164

Unless there are opportunities, when under training, to adopt the role, interact with others in that role, and thereby, to come to see the Self as constituted by the role, such training is likely to have little effect.

Second, if this sounds like an endorsement of the affective rather than cognitive emphasis of such courses, it is meant to. Many 'human relations' occupations and 'caring professions' seem intent upon imitating the established professions of law and medicine, by attempting to train new entrants in an esoteric body of definitive knowledge. Like AGs, they have turned to the social sciences to provide that body of knowledge and have been dismayed to find not certitude, but disputation. The error, however, is not only in believing that the social sciences are more definitive than they are, but also in believing that a Self can be taught. On the contrary, a Self can only be experienced, and, moreover, can only be experienced in interaction with others. By removing new entrants to such occupations from the operational context to a training school, the likelihood is that the opportunity to experience the Self as a member of the occupation is being denied and the socializing effect is, therefore, reduced, perhaps considerably. Of course, many of these occupations retain practical work 'placements' where students get the opportunity to experience themselves in their prospective role. Equally, it would be foolish to believe that all cognitive knowledge is inappropriate for these occupations. However, in the search for professional respectability the emphasis has been increasingly placed upon training in the classroom, which is an emphasis that may well prove to be misplaced.

NOTES

1. V.L. Olesen and E.W. Whittaker, The Silent Dialogue (San Francisco, Jossey-Bass, 1968).

AUTHOR INDEX

For Product Safety Concerns and Information please contact our EU
representative GPSR@taylorandfrancis.com
Taylor & Francis Verlag GmbH, Kaufingerstraße 24, 80331 München, Germany

www.ingramcontent.com/pod-product-compliance
Lightning Source LLC
Chambersburg PA
CBHW050446280326
41932CB00013BA/2263

9 781032 274614